THE BEST OF
BRITISH BUSES

Nº 10 Post~war REGENTS

ALAN TOWNSIN

The Transport
Publishing Company
128 Pikes Lane
Glossop Derbyshire
Tel: 045.74.61058

© Transport Publishing Company Ltd, August 1986

0 86317 131 1

TITLES IN THIS SERIES AND COMPANION VOLUMES

Illustrated list of all titles available on receipt of SAE

Typesetting, Artwork and Photography
by TPC Studio, Glossop, Derbyshire

Printed by Advertiser Press, Newport
Bound by John Sherratt & Son, Manchester
Colour work by Stott Bros, Halifax

Facing page.

Smartly turned out throughout its career with Bamber Bridge Motor Services, this 1954 AEC Regent III with East Lancashire bodywork is nowadays preserved and can again be seen looking much the same as in this scene about a quarter of a century ago. A synchromesh-gearbox model, its chassis number 9613S4922 filled one of the blanks left by a cancelled Nottingham order later switched to the Regent V. The choice of an AEC by an operator based a few miles from Preston and thus virtually on Leyland's doorstep was something of a triumph for AEC's sales department during those days of great rivalry. BBMS was taken over by Ribble in 1967 but this vehicle was not included in the sale.

Contents

Introduction

Not only bus enthusiasts but many drivers, mechanics and managers have a soft spot for the AEC Regent in one or other of its post-war forms, among which the London RT type is particularly prominent. This is partly simple nostalgia, compounded by the demise in 1979 of AEC itself, but it is also based on respect for a series of designs which combined technical advances with immense potential durability and ease of maintenance.

Even so, it is easy to forget just how successful was the Regent range, as built between 1945 and 1968. The total of over 13,000 vehicles built was second among double-deck types only to that of the Leyland Titan range which was its major rival. Inevitably the merger of AEC with Leyland in 1962 led to the overshadowing of the former by the latter, but the Regent's golden days had really ended with the close of the Regent III era in the mid 'fifties.

Though very much in tune with the down-to-earth needs of the immediate post-war period, the Regent II of 1945-47 was really the pre-war model in its final form with a mildly updated brake system. It was the Regent III that captured much of the industry's imagination, even though it took many of the 'non-believers' up to 20 years to accept that its key features—generous engine size, an air pressure brake system and transmission incorporating a fluid coupling and epicyclic gearbox—represented the logical way forward.

The credit for the Regent III must be shared to a large extent with London Transport. AEC had originally been set up specifically to build buses for London service and though the formation of LT in 1933 had broken the direct relationship, co-operation was to remain close until the 'sixties. The RT type had that characteristic blend of advanced concepts and severely practical detail work long typical of LT's Chiswick-based engineering department. It also looked 'right' in a way which meant that it still did not seem out of place on the streets 40 years after the first complete example appeared in 1939.

Yet the RT, and in particular its air brake system, might have seemed a troublesome white elephant had the war not provided time to overcome the shortcomings which are apt to be found when there is genuine innovation. As it was, by the time volume production got under way to meet London's large post-war need, it was a well-proved model, as demonstrated by the lack of major design changes during the manufacture of 4,674 post-war RT chassis for London service over the 1946-54 period.

AEC's provincial and export Regent III models gained from this solid production and design basis, even though differing both in appearance and, to a varying degree, in specification. When RT output ended in 1954, the combined total of over 8,000 post-war 9.6-litre Regent III models was several hundred in front of Leyland's output over the same period of the PD2 range (including London RTL and RTW as well as export versions).

Yet the huge London Transport business gave AEC a slightly 'unreal' advantage and when London's need for new buses temporarily collapsed, AEC output of double-deckers dropped quite sharply. Moreover, Chiswick was now demanding another technical leap forward with the Routemaster and AEC did not manage, this time, to reconcile it with pressure from other parts of the operating industry, notably the BET group, for a simpler and cheaper type of bus.

So the Regent V was introduced and virtually left to soldier on—even such promotional support as it got concentrated on the lightweight end of the range, yet it was the heavier version, more in the Mark III tradition, that was to be the long-term success, admittedly largely due to the need to introduce a 30ft. option. Exports played a much bigger part in the Mark V story, with the investment in properly designed left-hand models paying off to an unrivalled degree. In the event, the Regent V outsold its more technically advanced AEC stablemates, the Routemaster, Bridgemaster and Renown, taken together.

This book is intended as a record of some very solid achievements as well as a series of models that were favourite to many.

Basingstoke, 1986 Alan Townsin

Familiar to millions of London bus passengers, the 'face' of the RT conveyed the combination of advanced design and practicality that resulted from close and effective co-operation between AEC and its largest customer, London Transport. The vehicle seen here, RT1046, was based on quite an early chassis, O961441, and was among the first to receive a body without the roof-mounted route number box, in this case built by Weymann and, as often with that builder's RT production, painted green for use by the London Transport's country department, entering service in December 1948. Unusually, the early post-war livery with cream window surrounds is seen combined with a full destination display, not brought into regular use until 1950.

It is not easy to convey how strong an impression the arrival of a smart new batch of AEC buses complete with bodywork to high peacetime standards of appearance could be after the long drab war years. Newcastle Corporation's No. 28 (registered JVK 628) on chassis number O6617463 was one of the first three of that undertaking's initial post-war order for fourteen Regent II models to enter service, in January 1946. Half of the order had Weymann bodies of the elegant metal-framed style shown and the others Park Royal of a composite (wood-framed) type little removed from wartime practice. It was the former that caught the eye of the photographer of this scene the following month, showing No. 28 leaving the city terminus of route 13 to Wallsend, jointly operated with the Tyneside Tramways & Tramroads Co, one of whose 1939 ECW-bodied Leyland Titan TD5 can be seen in the background about to take up its position as the next bus on the route. Note the maze of trolleybus and tramway overhead.

Chapter one:
The Regent II, 1945-47

When AEC resumed the production of bus chassis just after the end of the World War 2 period, in the late summer of 1945, the new Regent double-decker models coming off the production line looked and sounded almost identical to those being turned out when manufacture had been stopped in 1941.

Officially, they were of a new type, the Regent II, but there was quite a lot in common even with the original Regent model of 1929, despite the lengthy list of revisions to the design that had occurred in the course of

building over 7,000 Regents up to 1941. That first version had been the brainchild of G. J. Rackham, who had been appointed Chief Engineer of the Associated Equipment Co Ltd, as it then was, the previous year (1928), and remained in that post until his retirement in 1950. He had been persuaded to leave the corresponding post at Leyland Motors Ltd, where he had just chalked up an immense success with the original Leyland Titan TD1 double-decker introduced in 1927, (see Nos. 1 and 7 of this series of books for more detail on Leyland

The continuity of development of the Regent from its earliest days is not difficult to detect from this picture (below left) of chassis number 661138, placed in service by Cornish Buses Ltd as its No. 69 (CV 1829) in 1930. The Short Bros bodywork was to the original standard 'camel-roof' AEC deisgn. The standard chassis design was progressively modernised in appearance and by November 1939, the radiator, bonnet and front mudguard were exactly as were to be used on post-war models, as is conveyed (below right) by this chassis picture, thought to show a Regal, the corresponding single-decker, of that date. The full story of the pre-1942 Regent models is told in No. 7 of this series.

Titans and AEC Regents respectively of the pre-1942 era).

The Regent of 1929 had much in common with the TD1, notably the use of a six-cylinder overhead-camshaft petrol engine in a chassis with sidemembers gracefully curved over the front and rear axles to give a lower floor line than hitherto usual. An offset and inclined transmission line using an underslung worm-drive rear axle also aided that objective.

However, from its introduction the Regent had set new standards in compact front-end layout and neat and distinctive appearance. This continued unaltered in essentials, as did the characteristic frame profile. Although details of the radiator, bonnet and front mudguards had altered, it was possible to update even the earliest models to Regent II standards of appearance, by a process of simple bolt-on substitution. In practice this was rarely applied to Regents but was quite common practice on the corresponding Regal single-deckers (fully described in No. 6 of this series).

On the other hand, AEC had generally kept up with contemporary trends and indeed helped to establish some with the many revisions to the original design. It is perhaps easiest to convey the mixed design age of the Regent II by examining the origins of its major units. The official drawing office designation of the type was O661/20, the 1941 version having been O661/19.

The engine was the A173 direct-injection six-cylinder diesel (invariably 'oil engine', in those days) always best known as the 7.7-litre — in conversation simply the 'seven-seven' — though its actual swept volume was 7.58 litres. This was the result of a decision made soon after its

A171 predecessor had been introduced, to reduce the bore size from 106mm to 105mm, the stroke remaining at a relatively long 146mm. The A171, which was of indirect-injection type, had first appeared in Regent chassis in 1934, becoming standard in 1935. The more efficient but less powerful A173 had been introduced as an option, without publicity, in 1936 but had become officially standard in 1939. In the form used in the Regent II its official power rating was 98 bhp at 1800 rpm, but some operators still favoured the economy 86 bhp setting which had been usual in wartime.

The A173 had helped to set a trend for engines using the toroidal-cavity type of combustion chamber in the top of the piston. Saurer had pioneered this in Switzerland and on the British Armstrong-Saurer in 1934, followed by Dennis, but AEC's version had become easily the most widely used in Britain by 1939. The A173 had been developed

largely as an answer to the Gardner 5LW 85 bhp five-cylinder engine of 7.0-litres capacity that had been setting new standards of fuel economy in buses by the mid-thirties, and though it never quite did as well, AEC's 7.7 DI unit (as it was also sometimes known) was regarded as one of the more efficient engines of its day.

The engine was also reliable and lasted well if not over-stressed, a fact underlined by its success in the famous AEC Matador 4 x 4 model built in huge numbers as a medium artillery tractor during the war, and much favoured as a recovery vehicle in the post-war years. The 7.7 had remained in production throughout the war and had also been used in Daimler and Bristol double-deck chassis built under the wartime utility bus programme as well as ERF and Maudslay goods chassis for civilian use. Hence it had become one of the best-known engines in its class. Even more significant was

the 'flattery by imitation' factor. Leyland's new 7.4-litre engine, as used in the PD1 double-decker, had clearly been developed to counter its success, sharing much the same size and having many features in common, while Dennis copied the exact cylinder dimensions for its post-war O6 oil engine.

The transmission was of older origin, with a single-plate clutch, four-speed gearbox and fully-floating rear axle. The D124 gearbox was essentially as introduced in 1931, with constant-mesh third gear of a curious design in which longshaft and mainshaft gears were both moved together along their respective shafts to allow the dog clutches to be engaged. The actual gears were of the same straight-toothed pattern as used from 1929 and, in operation, the typical AEC gear whine was unmistakeable. From a nostalgic viewpoint it nowadays seems a rather appealing sound, but by 1945 the unit was noisier than those of most competitors' models and sounded rather old-fashioned. The rear axle was largely as introduced for 1933 and the worm-and-nut steering dated from 1931. All these units had proved robust and reliable, and AEC's steering in particular was well-known for its lightness, partly as the result of low gearing.

Many of the features had been developed to suit London bus operation, AEC having originally been formed as the chassis-building subsidiary of the London General Omnibus Co Ltd. Though that relationship had ceased when AEC was set up as an independent business on the formation of London Transport in 1933, close association between AEC at Southall and the LT engineering headquarters at Chiswick, about three miles away, continued. Over half the

Regents built up to 1941 had been for operation in London. The bus design policy of London Transport had moved on quite a long way from the largely 1933 concept which the Regent II represented, apart from its engine, as will be described in the next chapter, but the general durability was well established.

The AEC Sales Department's choice of title 'Regent II' for the post-war chassis was not very logical, although not quite so inept as the corresponding use of Regal II for the equivalent single-decker, which had to be hastily amended to Regal I because a previous quite different model had used that designation.

There had been numerous variations of the pre-war Regent chassis between 1929 and 1941, all simply called 'Regent'. Some were far more important than the quite minor difference between the final standard 'plain' Regent (apt to be retrospectively called Regent I) as built in 1940-41, type O661/19, and the Regent II of 1945-47, type O661/20.

The only mechanical distinction between these latter types was the braking system, in both cases of vacuum-servo type, but actuated through a Lockheed hydraulic system on O661/19 (as on most earlier Regents since about 1932) whereas the O661/20 used the so-called triple-servo system which had come back into favour by 1945. In fact the name was rather misleading as the front brakes were applied by large vacuum cylinders piped to the main chassis-mounted servo. Leyland and Bristol used very similar systems, all based on Clayton Dewandre operating units.

The frame of the Regent II was as used on pre-war Regents ever since the 16ft. 3in. wheelbase had been adopted as standard in 1932-33 (following the

appearance of early examples in 1931) and in essentials had changed little since the original 15ft. 6½in. wheelbase version of 1929. The London General Omnibus Co Ltd had marked that distinction by a change of its type code from ST to STL and London Transport, continuing the same system, quite logically classified the 20 Regent II buses it received as STL type.

The outward appearance was unchanged from that of a standard O661/19-type bus, indeed it was largely as had been introduced for 1938 models, but with a vertically-slatted radiator grille and a reversion to an extensively louvred bonnet, both of which had first appeared at the end of 1939. The bonnet, in particular, was curiously dated-looking, being as used on most Regents of the 1932-37 period, and rather reminiscent of vintage Bentley practice.

Even so, the overall look of the chassis was attractive, with the polished finish of the handsome cast aluminium radiator and the front wheel-nut guard rings, plus a bonus that seemed particularly attractive after the years of dreary austerity, the chromium-plated engine oil filler cap visible through the access hole in the bonnet side.

On the road, the Regent II measured up quite well against the immediate post-war competition. The 7.7-litre engine was not outclassed in performance at a time when double-deckers generally had engines in the 85-100 bhp category and, although not particularly quiet or smooth-running, was at the time rather above average in both respects. The engine mounting system was of the pre-war standard Regent type, with just sufficient insulation to take off the edge of noise and vibration, but by no means a

When the Government agreed early in 1945 that AEC could resume bus production later that year, the London Passenger Transport Board naturally applied for an allocation, even though the model to be made available did not conform to its preferences, most notably in having the 'crash' gearbox. A batch of 20, all with Weymann bodywork, were allocated by the Ministry of War Transport, together with further Guy, Daimler and Bristol buses of more obviously wartime origin. Logically, the LPTB ignored AEC's rather artifical Regent II distinction, adding them to its STL class of 16ft. 3in.-wheelbase Regents which had been introduced in 1932. The numbers allocated, STL2682-2701, the last of the series, followed on from those given to 34 mechanically very similar Regents dating from 1941-42 and allocated at the beginning of the wartime system. The standard Weymann body design did not incorporate any of LPTB's usual bus characteristics, beyond such details as destination blinds and sidelamps, though there was some affinity in the styling to the quite different trolleybus department's ideas of the time. Seen here in original green and white livery with red oxide roof is STL2696 operating, like all 20 initially, from Watford garage — it was based on chassis O6617508, entering service in February 1946.

Liverpool Corporation's first post-war batch of sixteen Regent buses had bodywork to the same basic design as the other Weymann examples in the initial post-war batch, but they were sent to Liverpool's works at Edge lane for completion. As a result, they did not enter service until June-November 1946 though the chassis, O6617475-90, had all been completed by November 1945. Despite Liverpool having been a Weymann-bodied Regent user since 1935, the design, based on Weymann's immediate pre-war standard, was also unfamiliar in that city and the usual outswept skirt panels were evidently judged a little too elaborately curvaceous. The later batches which built up the total of Liverpool's Regent II fleet to 100 by late 1947 had a slightly simpler cab design.

flexible mounting as generally understood. The nature of the noise was less obtrusive than that from the contemporary 7.4-litre Leyland and the Regent was on the whole slightly quieter to ride in than either the Bristol K6A or Daimler CWA6 using the same AEC engine — the exhaust note was also well subdued.

Levels of engine vibration were apt to vary slightly between individual buses but the unpleasant out-of-balance thump found on some wartime AEC 7.7 engines was now very rarely detectable and it seemed that standards of manufacture had improved. On the other hand, an unfortunate 'grumbling' was apt to be heard from the transmission when running at about 20-25 mph, say if a driver was ahead of time. This had not been evident on pre-war models, but seemed to be common to both O661/20 and the corresponding Regal O662/20, persisting on subsequent Regent III models with the same crash-gearbox transmission, by then optional.

Mention of transmission options calls to mind the lack of any significant alternative specifications for the Regent II. This contrasted with the almost bewildering choice of AEC models of the late 'thirties. When AEC bus production restarted, this rigid standardisation was also true of other makes and was part of Government policy, under which operators had to accept approved wartime standards (still in force until the spring of 1946), but AEC continued this philosophy for the Regent II until the end, being in a position to resist operator pressure at a time of immense demand for new vehicles. Moreover, those who would have preferred preselective

transmission or a larger engine, both popular choices in 1939, could now be persuaded to take the Regent III, as described in the following chapters.

Regent II production

The initial announcement that AEC buses were once again to be made available was made shortly before the war ended, in March 1945, and operators were invited to apply for them under the Ministry of War Transport's allocation scheme. Several operators had already placed orders for post-war delivery, but these were treated separately and in at least two cases were fulfilled by the supply of Regent III models. In the event, 80 Regent II buses were supplied to British operators under the MoWT system. The chassis in question were numbered O6617451-7530, these numbers following immediately after 50 chassis built for Bombay in 1945

Delivery of these first 80 post-war AEC chassis to the bodybuilders was made between August 1945 and

January 1946 and bodybuilding was generally completed quite quickly, most of the vehicles being in service by about February 1946. They were allocated to Mansfield District Traction Co (ten vehicles), Newcastle Corporation (fourteen), Liverpool Corporation (sixteen), London Transport (20), Leicester Corporation (sixteen) and City of Oxford Motor Services (four), the chassis numbers being in that order.

Thus numerically the first chassis went to Mansfield, but examples were supplied almost simultaneously to several operators from December 1945. The bodywork contracts were split between Weymann and Park Royal, who respectively supplied 60 (of which the Liverpool 16 were supplied as shells) and 20 bodies. All were of 56-seat normal-height type but contrasted sharply otherwise, as Weymann reverted to its final pre-war metal-framed design of quite curvaceous style while Park Royal stuck to its wartime utility design relaxed only to a very slight degree.

The recipient of the last four of the true 'relaxed utility' Park Royal-bodied Regent II buses in the MoWT-allocated batch was City of Oxford Motor Services Ltd. The example which is seen ready to depart from Stratford-upon-Avon for Oxford with a full load in April 1950 is H304 (KFC 141) on chassis O6617529, which had been delivered in February 1946. The vehicle visible behind it is a Midland Red Daimler CWA6, GHA 994, Birmingham bound.

The return of normal direct ordering of vehicles resulted in more variety of body design, though the pressure on bodybuilders in particular meant that delivery tended if anything to become slower. Reading Corporation had been a regular customer for Park Royal-bodied Regents in pre-war days, but its need for lowbridge bodywork, with sunken side gangway in the upper deck, was fulfilled by this 50-seat metal-framed design. The chassis of No. 59 (CRD 253), O6617532 was one of three built in November 1945, followed closely by a further two but they were all combined with a further five built in August 1946 to form the basis of ten bodies completed in January-February 1947. By the time this picture was taken, the radiator had been exchanged for one from a pre-war Regent, by no means an uncommon happening.

The Mansfield, Liverpool and London Transport batches were all of the Weymann type, the Newcastle and Leicester batches were split between both builders and the Oxford buses were all Park Royal.

After that, body supply reverted to normal practice, quite a wide variety of builders becoming involved, as is conveyed by the illustrations. Most of the users, though not all, were traditional AEC customers. The Weymann design was built on quite a large scale, with further batches for some of the above-mentioned concerns and several others, generally subsidiaries of the BET group, but

some Regent II chassis went to most of the better-known double-deck bodybuilders of the day, as well as some less familiar. Chassis construction went ahead rapidly, deliveries continuing throughout 1946 and being completed by the end of 1947, some 645 examples being built with chassis numbers running up to O6618095, though chassis deliveries were not strictly in sequence, among the last being part of an Oxford batch with numbers up to O6617919.

Body manufacture began to slip behind in several cases due to the immense pressure of demand, but the majority of Regent II buses were in

The war had some curious consequences, among them being the appearance in 1946 of thirteen new Regent II chassis in the fleet of the Western Welsh Omnibus Co Ltd, with Eastern Coach Works bodywork that had been built to pre-war design for an order for sixteen Regent buses (eight lowbridge and eight of conventional centre-gangway highbridge layout) of which only two lowbridge buses had been delivered, in October 1940. One highbridge body had been mounted on an 'unfrozen' Regent chassis, in 1942, but the remainder had somehow evaded the usual wartime procedures under which any 'spare' body or chassis were completed and put to use, by no means necessarily for the intended purchaser. Thus chassis number 06617540 is seen here after receiving one of the six lowbridge bodies and becoming No. 617 (CKG 797). Comparison of this official ECW picture with one of the two 1940 buses on page 145 of the author's more general history of AEC buses 'Blue Triangle', also published by TPC, indicates that the original cab to suit the slightly taller 8.8-litre bonnet had not been altered. The 'British Buses' symbols formed part of an advertising campaign by company operators opposing nationalisation.

Midland Red had only six AEC buses in its fleet — Regent models allocated under wartime agreements in 1942 — when 100 Regent II were ordered for the early post-war period. Own-make BMMO chassis would have been preferred — Midland Red had not placed a bulk order for 'bought-out' buses in peacetime since the 'twenties — but the standard 0661/20 chassis design was accepted. (The company's Carlyle works was fully occupied with the new underfloor-engine single-deckers for which nothing equivalent was available elsewhere). However, the appearance, with full-width bonnet, was to be as on a BMMO prototype double-decker, type D1, built in 1944, the new Regents being designated AD2 within Midland Red. The body contract was split between Brush and Metro-Cammell and it was hoped that delivery would begin in 1946, but did not start until 1948 and in the case of the Metro-Cammell batch extended to 1950, making these the last Regent II buses to enter service. The styling contrasted oddly with the traditional sound effects from the gearbox in particular. Seen here is the first, Brush-bodied, vehicle when new — No. 3100 (JHA 1) was on chassis O6617661.

Enterprise & Silver Dawn Motor Services Ltd was a more substantial independent operator than its romantic-sounding title might suggest, operating well over 100 vehicles in the Scunthorpe area. Most were AEC Regal single-deckers, but double-deck operation had begun in wartime and five Regent II buses with lowbridge 55-seat Burlingham bodywork were added to the fleet in 1946, No. 20 (DBE 969) seen here being on chassis O6617726. Two more generally similar buses but of highbridge layout were added in 1947 but the business, by then Enterprise (Scunthorpe) Ltd sold out to the Lincolnshire Road Car Co Ltd in 1950.

The Northern General Transport Co Ltd had been a regular AEC customer since the early 'thirties. Its last new Regents, the only post-1945 deliveries, were ten dating from the latter part of 1946 and carrying 56-seat bodywork by the local concern, Northern Coachbuilders. Number 1168 (ACN 168), on chassis O6617891, is seen in South Shields on the Newcastle service. Thereafter, the Guy Arab with Gardner 5LW engine became NGT's favoured double-decker until the late 'fifties.

The Western SMT Co Ltd, on the other hand, had generally favoured Leyland buses but the immediate post-war deliveries after the completion of wartime allocations were AEC models. A batch of 30 Regent II models with Northern Counties 53-seat lowbridge bodywork was delivered in 1946-47. Fleet numbers were not then in use and BAG 124, on chassis O6617750, seen here in Glasgow, was one of those delivered in 1946, remaining in service until 1961. Northern Counties bodies had been introduced to this fleet in wartime and the Wigan firm was to be a regular supplier thereafter.

Weymann was easily the most popular choice of bodywork for the Regent II, some 305 of the 645 chassis produced receiving bodywork of the classic design shown, including the 100 delivered in shell form for completion by Liverpool for its own use. Almost all were highbridge and seated 56, though Hull's fifteen accommodated 60 (an idea adopted from wartime Regents with Brush bodywork diverted from Coventry), while 20 of the total were of lowbridge pattern (fifteen for South Wales and five for Midland General). The example seen here in Nottingham in 1950 is one of Midland General's highbridge examples, No. 60 (KNU 601) on chassis O6617734, one of eight delivered in 1946, remaining in service until 1962.

Eastern Coach Works Ltd, though mainly occupied in supplying bodywork to the Tilling group of companies, of which it was a member, was able at that stage to accept orders from other concerns for designs based on its contemporary standard products. The local municipal operator, Lowestoft, naturally turned to this source for eight 56-seat double-deckers on Regent II chassis in 1947. Seen in the town centre is No. 25 (GBJ 196), on chassis O6617949. One further body to virtually the same specification was built on a Regent II for an independent operator, the Ebor Bus Co of Mansfield, the same year.

City of Oxford Motor Services Ltd followed up its allocation of four Park Royal-bodied Regents delivered at the beginning of 1946 with 21 more supplied in the autumn of that year, including H325 (LWL 320) on chassis O6617871 (seen above). The body design was derived from the wartime timber-framed structure but incorporated refinements such as radiused window corners and a slightly more harmonious rear dome outline, being quite closely related to the style used for 100 Daimler CWA6 for London Transport. There was a shortage of destination equipment at the time and these buses were delivered with the aperture temporarily panelled over, painted-on destinations being used as shown (above right) by another vehicle of the same batch.

The Park Royal concern, not then financially associated with AEC, built only a relatively small proportion of the bodywork for the Regent II. Though of several types there were 71 vehicles in all, of which only six were of what was possibly the best-known Park Royal design of the period, the metal-framed highbridge style built in large numbers especially on Guy chassis. They were built for Morecambe & Heysham Corporation, entering service in 1947. The vehicle seen here was No. 8 (GTJ 693) on chassis O6617874.

service by 1948. The last are believed to have been 50 vehicles from a fleet of 100 built for the Midland Red concern, then officially the Birmingham & Midland Motor Omnibus Co Ltd. The chassis were built in two batches, of 65 and 35 respectively, O6617695-7723 and O6617775-7809, all completed between May 1946 and January 1947. All were supplied without bonnet or front wings and with a 'plain' rather than styled radiator to suit Midland Red's full-width bonnet style as pioneered on a prototype own-make double-decker built in 1944. The 56-seat bodies, also to BMMO style, were split equally between Brush, which delivered its 50 in 1948, and Metro-Cammell; the latter had produced only one in 1949 and the rest in 1950, some chassis having thus awaited bodying for almost four years. Midland Red had used AEC oil

engines in its own chassis in the mid-'thirties and for wartime conversions of petrol-engined buses, but these were almost its only vehicles based on complete AEC chassis. The non-supply of the more visible parts of the usual front-end was the only instance of a fairly major departure from the Regent II standard design.

Midland Red shared the distinction of running the largest fleet of Regent II models with Liverpool Corporation which also had 100, in additon to a pre-war fleet on basically similar Regent chassis. On the other hand, several important Regent customers had none of the Mark II variety. Both Glasgow and Leeds among municipal fleets, and Devon General and Rhondda among companies, preferred to wait for the Regent III.

The intention to build a version of the

Regent III to cater for operators favouring the main mechanical features of the Regent II, and thus replacing that model, had been revealed by published specification lists early in 1947, so the ending of production came as no surprise. It occurred without ceremony or fuss and yet the end of the type 661 closed an era that had lasted for eighteen years.

Trent Motor Traction Co Ltd built up a fleet of 55 AEC Regent II buses in the 1946-48 period, all with Willowbrook bodywork. The last 30, delivered in 1948, included ten lowbridge versions but the remainder were of the style shown; No. 1158 (ACH 648) on chassis O6618049 still has that 'new' look as it stands outside the Trent garage in Loughborough, the town where the bodywork was built, in July 1949. Willowbrook's outline, with sloping rather than curved profile, was rather conservative for the period but the particularly neat window treatment and Trent's distinctive red and white livery produced a smart effect.

Cardiff Corporation took delivery of nineteen Regent II. The first of them, O6617841, is seen just after delivery in 1947 as No. 95 (CUH 371). The body, to East Lancashire's restrained yet stylish design, was built by Air Dispatch (Coachbuilders) Ltd, a Cardiff concern later known as Bruce Coach Works Ltd, and one of several 'offshoot' enterprises with which East Lancs was to be associated over the years. Air Dispatch built six of the bodies in this batch, all being of 56-seat highbridge type, in 1947-48 and nine more in 1948 but the remaining four, 53-seat lowbridge buses, were bodied by East Lancs at its Blackburn works in 1947.

The final batch of Regent II models, in numerical terms, was O6618086-95, of which the chassis were built for Reading Corporation between March and June 1947, although several batches with earlier numbers for other operators were built later that year. Park Royal built the 52-seat lowbridge bodywork, delivering the completed vehicles in September 1948, and although basically similar to that of the earlier batch shown on page 10, these reverted to this operator's pre-war practice in having half-drop windows with continuous rain louvre, 'square-cut' at the front corners, and thus had a more old-fashioned appearance than their predecessors. It was an odd quirk of fate that Reading had both the last 661-series Regent and later the last 681-series bus, the latter being the last Regent III of all, as explained on page 53. The vehicle seen here, No. 81 (CRD 870) was on chassis O6618093, the last but two of a series that had begun in 1929.

AEC's publicity department had skilfully kept up operators' interest in the RT-type throughout the war period. This photograph of RT53, one of the initial production batch of 150 buses, had been used in press articles and advertisements, the latter now referring to the new model as the Regent Mark III. The London Transport fleetname and bonnet number had been touched out, but the background, with LT-type six-wheel buses visible, quite apart from the reference to 55, Broadway, SW1, on the destination blind and indeed the unmistakable architecture of the bodywork (built within the LPTB's Chiswick works visible behind) left no room for doubt. This particular bus had entered service in March 1940.

Chapter two:
The post-war RT, 1946-50

AEC had kept up its publicity and advertising activities to a greater extent than most manufacturers during the war years. Most concerns vaguely referred to renewed availability of vehicles when the war ended but AEC was more specific, with descriptive material on the Regent RT-type, as it was called up to about 1943. Public references to the new model as the

Regent Mark III seem to have begun with an advertising campaign in the technical press towards the end of 1944, although internal use of this name, and references to it in conversations to operators, probably began earlier.

The early story of the RT model is told in Chapter Six of the author's 'AEC Regents 1929-42', which is No. 7

in the same series as this volume, and also in Chapter Eight of his more general book on AEC buses, 'Blue Triangle'. Briefly, it stemmed from London Transport's decision to adopt a 'big engine' policy for a new double-decker of advanced design, made as far back as 1937. At the time, the London Passenger Transport Board (to quote the full name adopted on its

This view of part of the chassis of O6616750, better known as RT2, taken before bodying late in 1939, shows some of the key features of the model and also its one major weakness at that stage. Prominent is the 9.6-litre A185 engine and its rear rubber mounting, surrounding the front end of the propeller shaft. Just to the right of this is the diminutive rotary air compressor, driven by a separate small-diameter propeller shaft from the front end of the engine, in tandem with the dynamo, for which this location and method of drive was well-established London Transport practice. The compressor proved to be unreliable and inadequate for the job; the amount of high-pressure air needed for the brakes and the air-operated preselective gearbox under city conditions had simply been under-estimated. A bigger two-cylinder reciprocating compressor was found to solve the problem and was fitted to this and other chassis in the later war period, as well as being standardised for post-war production.

The September 1945 issue of 'AEC Gazette' included this report of the display in July of the chassis of RT19, by then modified so as to become the prototype for the post-war version. All but one of the operators whose senior management were shown to be present in this and another picture later bought Regent Mark III buses, often in substantial numbers in relation to the sizes of fleet concerned — the BET group, Midland General, the municipalities of Liverpool, Sheffield, Brighton, St. Helens and Edniburgh (though the last-mentioned admittedly bought only one batch). The sole non-buyer, Yorkshire (Woollen District), became a Regent V user in later years. It is noteworthy that the engine, though internally to post-war specification, had a non-standard shape of valve-cover — production versions were to revert nearer to the pre-war outline.

Above. Left to right: Mr. S. Hollands (A.E.C.); Mr. Raymond Birch (B.E.T. Federation); Mr. R. McLeod (Edinburgh); Mr. Winston Robinson (Brighton) and Mr. G. W. Robb (St. Helens).

The "Regent Mark III"

Leading Transport Officials Look Over A.E.C.'s Post-War Luxury Bus Chassis

Municipal managers and heads of the large company-owned undertakings, in London for the annual general meetings of the M.P.T.A. and the P.T.A. in July, had the opportunity of inspecting the A.E.C. " Regent " Mark III when a chassis of this type was placed on view at a convenient point in the Central London area.

formation in 1933) was adding large numbers of AEC Regents with 7.7-litre engines to its fleet, this model being the basis of the LPTB's STL-class double-decker, as mentioned in the previous chapter.

However, AEC's standard oil engine up to 1935 was an 8.8-litre unit, the A165, still available on request, and this had been used in a large-scale programme in which six-wheel double-deckers of the LPTB's LT-class, based on AEC Renown chassis dating from 1931-32, were converted from petrol. London Transport engineers had also been impressed with Leyland's 8.6-litre engine, a direct-injection engine of unusually smooth-running character and the eventual outcome after two intermediate stages was the development of a new engine retaining the 142mm stroke dimension of the 8.8-litre unit, but with bore increased from 115mm to 120mm to give the 9.6-litre swept volume that was to become so familiar. This was type A185, with Leyland-style combustion system, deliberately derated to give 100 bhp at 1800 rpm, hardly any more than could have been obtained from the direct-injection 7.7-litre.

It was installed in a new 16ft. 4in.-wheelbase chassis differing in many ways from the standard Regent of the time, though included in the same O661 chassis number series. The frame differed in shape, both in plan view and in such details as the dumb-iron outline, more upright than previously. Mechanically there were many new features but perhaps the most important was the use of an air-

pressure system to operate both the brakes (a feature commonplace on trolleybuses but previously rare on motor buses in Britain) and the preselective gearbox. The latter was basically of the Wilson type, used in conjunction with a fluid flywheel as on many AEC and Daimler buses already in service but with a much lighter gear-change pedal action thanks to the air operation and being controlled by a new steering-column mounted selector lever. There was also a very effective flexible engine mounting and the whole front-end design was remarkably compact, accommodating the large-capacity engine in virtually the same bonnet length as needed for the 7.7 and having a lower bonnet height to improve driver vision.

The prototype, O6616749, had been numbered RT1 in April 1939 after receiving its intended sleek-looking four-bay body (it had operated with an old body and been given the deliberately misleading number ST1140 for a few months in 1938) but did not enter public service as RT1 until 9th August 1939, less than a month before war was declared on 3rd September. The production batch of 150 buses numbered RT2-151 on chassis O6616750-6899 did not begin to enter service until January 1940, the last one not doing so until February 1942.

One of the first of these, RT19, registered FXT 194, had been in service for only three weeks when it was hired back to AEC for use as a demonstrator in February 1940. It visited numerous operators in almost all parts of Britain and was retained by

AEC until August 1942, latterly being painted green. It then returned to London Transport service restored to standard red livery but was again selected for special treatment in March 1945, just as AEC's plans for resumed bus production were being announced. It went back to AEC again but this time without body (its original body being transferred to RT66, which had suffered air raid damage).

The chassis of RT19 was modified to a specification very similar to the post-war standard, with engine still of 9.6-litre capacity but with the toroidal type of direct injection as used on the A173 7.7-litre engine, among other minor changes. It seems very probable that RT19 was selected for this purpose because of its earlier spell in AEC's charge. Considerable development work had been done to improve the reliability of the RT-type buses in service during 1940-42 when RT19 would have been available to try out modifications, doubtless retaining those that proved beneficial.

Reliability, in later years to be regarded as one of the RT's most important virtues, had not been a strong point at first. Though the basic concept, and especially the philosophy of a lightly-stressed engine, was sound, the designers ran into the type of problem faced by many pioneers, notably with the air system. The compressor proved to be particularly troublesome, resulting in a completely different type being adopted. The war turned the initial RT fleet into a large-scale development exercise and by 1945 most of the problems had been solved with immense benefit to post-war users.

The modified chassis of RT19 was shown to general managers of many of the more prominent municipal and company fleets when they attended trade association meetings in London in July 1945 and was returned to London Transport the following month. It was then fitted with the Chiswick-built metal-framed body from the original 1939 prototype, RT1, this being nearer to the LPTB's proposed new standard than the 150 bodies dating from 1940-41 which were of composite (timber-framed) construction. The chassis of RT1, which had brake units of types for

When RT19's chassis was returned to London Transport's Chiswick works in August 1945 following its updating at Southall, plus the publicity exercise shown opposite, it received the body from RT1. This approximated to the intended post-war standard in its largely metal-framed construction and in particular in the cantilevered rear end, with platform carried from the body structure without support from the chassis. It returned to service in November 1945, being officially classified as of type 3RT1, in other words with post-war type 3RT chassis and RT1-type body. It then continued in service and when overhauled in 1951 re-emerged again retaining this body, as shown here, though by then in what had become standard livery with only one cream band. The mudguards were of post-war type, but the mouldings were still of the ribbed type peculiar to this body from its original construction in April 1939 — there were several other minor differences, including a slightly more 'severe' look to the upper-deck front windows. Fortunately the body was to survive after withdrawal from pasenger service in 1955 — see page 89.

which spares were unobtainable, was dismantled in 1946, but RT19 re-entered service in November 1945.

It had been intended from the beginning that London Transport would place large numbers of RT-type buses in service and the initial production order of 150 placed in July 1938 had been followed up by a further 188 in November of that year, not fulfilled due to the war. Indeed, there was the intention of ordering at least 1,000, eventually, behind the original plans. With a greatly increased need for new buses due to the war, a formal agreement to supply 1,000 RT-type chassis as soon as improved circumstances allowed was made with AEC by the LPTB in April 1944, a couple of months before the Allied armies regained the D-day foothold on the Continent of Europe and the war

thus still far from won. Further orders of similar size were expected to follow, and by January 1945, with the invasion of Europe well established and the end of the war expected soon, AEC was hoping to begin delivery by the end of the year.

Meanwhile, the new model had awakened interest among many other operators, both traditional AEC users and others. The demonstration tour of RT19 in the early wartime period was intended to encourage orders from operators outside London and thereby help to recover the development costs from larger numbers of chassis. By about 1941, it was becoming quite common practice to order buses for post-war delivery and so far as AEC was concerned such orders were largely associated with the Regent Mark III, described simply as 'the

Post-war Bus' in the advertisements of 1944 onwards.

Wartime controls on manufacture required Ministry of War Transport approval for firm orders for new buses while mere reservations for post-war supply, without specific date, were handled rather differently. The MoWT was involved in the early stages of the post-war London RT orders and may have played a part in other early Regent III chassis allocations. AEC practice was to allocate chassis numbers on receipt of order, not necessarily related to the sequence in which the chassis were built. The return of normality inevitably took place unevenly and some bodybuilders could resume normal production more quickly than others, quite apart from operators' own varying circumstances.

The Regent III was given a new type

This drawing of an O961-type chassis dates from November 1946 and was intended for use in a lubrication chart. It shows how the RT-type frame had two parallel portions rather than tapering from the middle all the way to the front dumb-irons as on the standard 661 and O661-type versions. Also clearly shown are the belt-driven arrangements for the dynamo and

compressor, the latter accounting for one of the characteristic RT sounds, something between a light tinkle and a rustling noise, that could be heard beneath the floor, falling silent if the vehicle was idling in gear, as the compressor was not then being driven. The 7mm scale drawing shows the short-tailed frame — the fuel tank, on the nearside, is omitted.

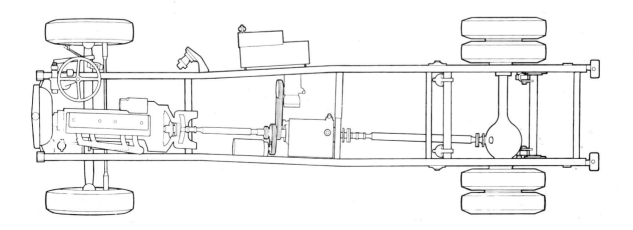

It came as quite a surprise that the first of the post-war O961-series Regent Mark III buses should go to West Riding Automobile Co Ltd rather than London Transport, for whom a pre-war RT order was still outstanding. West Riding had also been almost exclusively a Leyland customer in the 'thirties, standardising latterly on the Gearless models with torque converter transmission, and choice of transmission involving minimum driver effort was almost the only element of continuity. The nine chassis, numbered O961001-009, were delivered for bodying between May and August 1946. The vehicles were purchased for WR's former tram route from Leeds through Wakefield to Belle Isle, so they had centre-entrance twin-staircase bodywork by Roe and were painted in a red livery, as had been other vehicles for this route since

its conversion to bus operation in 1932 — the seating capacity was 50, with only 22 on the lower deck. Like other RT-type chassis supplied to provincial operators in 1946, they had bonnet top panels of London RT pattern but the front mudguards and lower bonnet sides were of a curiously amateurish style, the wings vaguely like those of a Regent II but looking as if designed to suit the 11.00-20 tyre size to be standard on the provincial Regent III rather than the high-pressure 9.00-20 which was London Transport's choice. It was unfortunate that the bus chosen for this official bodybuilder's picture taken in November 1946 was No. 61 (AHL 656) which was O961006, rather than No. 56, which was '001.

number, O961, unlike the RT-type models of the 1939-40 period, and in AEC's usual fashion the chassis numbers began at O961001. In view of London Transport's clear intention of continuing with its RT programme as soon as possible, it came as a surprise to find that the first post-war London order began at O961020, which chassis was delivered from AEC to the LPTB's Chiswick works on 26th March 1946. This initial batch ran to O961185, thus comprising 166 chassis, an odd number seemingly unrelated to either the 1944 order for 1,000 or the initial body contracts for 250 each from Park Royal and Weymann agreed in January 1946.

It seems possible that AEC's original plan might have been to build the 188 chassis outstanding from the November 1938 order, for the next batch of RT chassis for London

comprised 312 chassis (O961239-550), which would have brought the total to 500, thus matching the body order. A rather curious small batch of 22 further London RT chassis (O961587-608) did bring the total to the 500 and might well have been replacements for the 22 seemingly 'pinched' from the initial order.

However, the actuality brings in further complications. If the intention had been that O961001-188 would all have been London chassis, some at least were not built as such or even conformed to the London RT specifications. Half of the 'missing' 22 were built to the provincial Regent III specification, as described in the next chapter, but the order numbers indicate that all the chassis numbers in question were allocated at about the same time and construction of certain orders may have been held back and

then completed to provincial specification to suit the operators or bodybuilders.

It is noteworthy that chassis numbers O961189-238 (a total of 50) were all RT-type chassis supplied to various municipal and BET group operators and that the allocation of chassis numbers O961551 upwards for some export vehicles seems to have been made before any of the earlier O961-series numbers, suggesting that O961001-550 might all have been intended to be RT-type chassis, including 50 for operators outside London, before a general switch to the provincial type for non-London orders, including export examples.

As it turned out, chassis numbers O961001-009 were supplied to the West Riding Automobile Co Ltd of Wakefield, not hitherto an AEC customer, though it was to place

Grimsby Corporation had been a traditional customer for both AEC chassis and Roe bodywork, though its post-war orders called for relatively conventional rear-entrance design, with 56 seats, rather than the centre-entrance layout, first applied to a double-decker on a Regent built by Roe for this fleet in 1930. This body style was very largely as first seen earlier in 1946 on the first Leyland PD1 double-deckers. However, Roe had not previously been involved in a design where the whole cab from floor-level upwards was the bodybuilder's responsibility and though the end result was quite neat, there were some demarcation problems in just where chassis and body makers' responsibilities extended. The original plan had been that the bonnet and front wings were to be supplied by the bodybuilder; this was evidently abandoned, but it may account for the slightly odd detail work — note that in this case the valance over the offside dumb iron is actually a separate plate, riveted to the cab front. Number 82 (JV 9902) on chassis O961216 was one of three buses, all placed in service in mid-December. Halifax received eight almost identical buses the same month.

Another early recipient of post-war RT-type buses was Aberdeen Corporation, No. 17 (BRS 517) being the first of its batch of ten though on numerically the last chassis, O961213. It is seen here in winter sunshine at Southall after bodying by Weymann and before delivery in time to enter service in December 1946. The 56-seat body was a four-bay version of Weymann's contemporary standard, suiting the chassis well except that the front bulkhead had its window sill level about 9in. higher than would have best suited the RT bonnet level. The headlamps, as used on early post-war London RT deliveries, were of an unusual, rather crude-looking, style with the offside lamp mounted lower than the nearside one.

Birmingham City Transport received the biggest single batch of the RT-type chassis supplied to provincial operators in 1946-47. Number 1631 (GOE 631), on chassis number O961200, being seen here at Southall after bodying by Park Royal but before delivery, was the first of the fifteen to enter service, in August 1947 — the chassis had been built nearly a year earlier. By mid-1947, London Transport's belated deliveries had begun and the other provincial operators' examples were almost all in service, so the styling, decidedly eccentric at any date, seemed completely at odds with accepted practice, particularly for this chassis. The 54-seat body shell was based on Park Royal's new four-bay design as developed for the provincial Regent III and illustrated on page 30 but with the front end modified to incorporate BCT's contemporary reversion to a typical early 'thirties windscreen angle, the aim being to eliminate night-time reflection problems. Details of finish were to BCT's usual high standards and unladen weight a rather high 7 tons 16 cwt.

Devon General Omnibus & Touring Co Ltd placed eight RT-type models in service in February 1947. The Weymann bodywork was much the same as had been supplied to Aberdeen but had the benefit of this bodybuilder's traditional outswept skirt panels, which suited the design well. Another BET company, Rhondda Transport Ltd, had received five buses to the same design in December 1946. Devon General's DR 327 (HTT 327), on chassis O961219, is seen in Newton Abbott in company with another bus of the same batch when about ten years old. Both buses are in DG's usual smart condition, and an interesting modification was the fitting of larger front tyres, as shown.

The strangest story concerning the 'provincial' RT buses was that of Coventry Corporation's solitary example. The chassis O961217, was among the earliest to be delivered, on 4th July 1946, and although engine numbers were not strictly in sequence, it is noteworthy that it had A204 engine No. 2 (the first London chassis, O961020, having had No. 1). The body was to be built by Metro-Cammell and it was expected — or feared — that this might have a Birmingham-style profile as adopted for Coventry's contemporart Daimler buses. But Metro-Cammell adopted a policy of basing production on a limited number of designs to minimise delay and the solitary RT chassis was an odd-man-out, languishing unused until London Transport awarded the firm a contract to body 450 Leyland RTL-type buses. London Transport's policy of requiring the Leyland chassis to conform exactly to the RT body dimensions meant that Coventry's chassis would accept this design of body, so an extra body was added at the end of the London order. The completed bus was first licensed on 1st March 1951, the chassis then being 4¾ years old.

Despite the conformity to London RT standards, Metro-Cammell's method of mounting kept the London bodies on their original Leyland chassis (RTL551-1000) and Coventry's No. 99 was thus to remain the only AEC RT chassis with a Metro-Cammell body, broadly conforming to London coding 3RT7 had such a combination existed, though the body incorporated Coventry indicators and the chassis an offside fuel tank, unlike London's nearside standard. It received complete RT-type wings etc, but a curious oddity was the 'Regent' script title on the radiator, fitted from new and thought to be the only one on an RT-type chassis. It remained in service at Coventry until 1964.

'The new RT buses are wondrous things'. When they first appeared in London's streets in 1947, the post-war RT-types had a dramatic visual impact in a city still bearing numerous scars of the war years and with most other vehicles on the streets looking rather shabby. The design looked dramatically modern — and indeed subsequently never seemed to date as other more ephemeral fashions came and went. There is no such thing as perfection and the author was never happy about the relationship between the sill levels of the windscreen and side windows on the post-war version, but it was indeed a classic design having immense influence on a variety of later designs. RT168, based on chassis number O961125, gleams in the sun at Park Royal before being delivered to Chiswick works and being prepared for entry into service from Leyton garage in September 1947.

regular orders for Regent III buses until 1952. I was fortunate enough to pay my first visit to the works of Charles H.Roe Ltd while the bodies on these and other very early Regent III chassis for Grimsby (O961214-6) and Halifax (O961231-2) were under construction in about October 1946 and recall hearing of the bodybuilder's problems in building on London RT-type chassis, which lacked the usual dash panels and lower half of the cab. It seems that seven of the West Riding buses, including O961001, were delivered in November 1946 and thus were the first Regent III models to enter service, beating the Grimsby and Halifax buses which dated from December, as did O961225-9 with Weymann bodies for the Rhondda fleet.

It had been intended that delivery of bodied post-war RT-type buses for London Transport would begin in July 1946, before any of the buses for provincial fleets mentioned above. However, London Transport's decision to adopt aircraft standards of construction for the bodywork, with much closer tolerances than hitherto

usual and extensive use of gauges to check this caused a delay of virtually a year before production got under way. Construction was delegated to 'outside' bodybuilders, Chiswick works being much too heavily occupied with repair and overhaul. The aim was complete interchangeability of parts between Park Royal and Weymann bodywork, and chassis also had to conform to

an elaborate jig, checking critical points where the body would fit. The supply of RT chassis from AEC filled up all available storage space at the bodybuilders and at various London Transport garages, eventually forcing a pause in production of some five months from the end of 1946, despite the desperate need for new buses in service, though other AEC customers

The delays in bodybuilding produced a sizeable 'pool' of unused London RT-type chassis and several of the first batch were temporarily diverted to other uses. Possibly the strangest was O961079, fitted with an open-staircase body from one of the ST-class Regents dating from 1930-31 that had been taken over from Thomas Tilling Ltd in 1933, and used as an engineering training vehicle with the chassis number as its fleet number and on trade plates until 1954, when it finally emerged with a new Weymann body as RT 4761, (OLD 548). Note the vaguely RT-pattern cab.

Familiar to millions of Londoners for a quarter of a century — and even longer in some cases — the interior of the post-war RT was almost unchanged from that of the prototype vehicles as introduced in 1939. The characteristic curved pressings used as window finishes were widely copied, though rarely styled so effectively. The continuation of the sill level from the side windows across the front bulkhead gave an airy effect. This view of an early Park Royal-bodied example was taken in that bodybuilder's yard before delivery in the later part of 1947. Some of the many RT chassis awaiting bodying are visible and, on the left, one of the British Overseas Airways Commer airport coaches.

(Left) By comparison, a typical 'provincial' Regent III of the type described in the next chapter had forward vision restricted by the high bulkhead sill level. This is one of the lowbridge RLH-type buses diverted to London Transport from a Midland General order. The characteristic Weymann design, with both upper and lower edges of the bulkhead windows curved, did slightly mitigate the effect and also had the virtue that the driver could look back into the bus more easily.

The author's favourite seat for a bus ride round London gave this excellent view forward over the RT-type bonnet while settled back into the comfortably upholstered seat, even if the leg room in the front was rather cramped ....

.... while the driver had a truly commanding view, with his seat cushion just about at bonnet level. The preselector lever was nicely placed just below the steering wheel. Both these views show preserved RT1379.

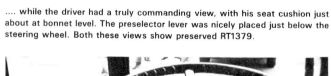

benefitted from the diversion of attention to their orders.

The first complete post-war RT was eventually delivered to Chiswick from Weymann's on 28th April 1947 and the first from Park Royal a fortnight later. They were respectively numbered RT402 and RT152, these numbers being the first of the batches of 250 each from the two bodybuilders. No attempt was made to keep the chassis numbers in sequence as had been the case or the 'pre-war' RT buses and RT402 was on chassis O961096 while RT152 was on O961031. London Transport's policy in this respect was somewhat illogical, indeed, as although fleet numbers were related to bodybuilders' batches and the London Transport body numbers and registratio: numbers issued in sequence, the tie-up with the body number was broken as soon as bodywork was transferred at overhaul. Chassis were drawn from stock as required, regardless of number, and the delay inevitably caused the relationship between the chassis and fleet numbers to be not merely out of sequence but intermingled between widely separated batches. Some early chassis were temporarily diverted to training and other duties, an example being 0961037 which did not enter service until December 1949, as RT2436.

This was partly because the standardisation of the AEC chassis in particular was remarkably tight. London Transport's type code system uses prefix numbers for chassis variations and all the post-war RT chassis were 3RT, a code which had also been applied to RT19 when rebuilt in 1945 as the post-war prototype, the code for RT2-151 as built having been 2RT. There were minor modifications from time to time but none regarded as sufficient to justify departing from the 3RT chassis code. The corresponding body code for both Park Royal and Weymann bodies as built in 1947-48 was RT3, the complete vehicle being 3RT3, but the body codes successively changed with destination display and other revisions in design.

Despite the existence of the earlier RT fleet of generally similar appearance, the new RT buses seemed wondrous things in 1947. London Transport's fleet had suffered from the effects of the war to a greater degree than many others due to the regularity of air raids in its area, and shiny new buses of any kind would have stood out. But the RT's stylish design made most other double-deckers, new or otherwise, look dated and the careful thought given to all aspects of design became more evident on closer examination.

The post-war body, of much more durable construction that the 1940 version, largely accounted for a weight increase of 18 cwt to 7 tons 10 cwt, but the post-war engine, type A204, was set to give 115 bhp at the same 1800 rpm, enough to give a lively performance. Interior finish was neat and the seats comfortable (though in fairness the latter was equally true of most London buses built from 1936). A very effective flexible engine mounting system kept noise levels down and this tended, if anything, to improve after a couple of years' service. The air-operated brakes and gear-change pedal required less effort than the STL and the use of relatively small-section front tyres as preferred by London Transport kept the steering lightness of earlier models.

On the other hand there were two features out of line with accepted contemporary practice. The engine had no external air cleaner and there were no shock absorbers, more correctly described as dampers, on the leaf springs. Both reflected London conditions, the amount of dust in the air evidently not being reckoned to require filtration beyond that given by a simple form of silencer built into the valve cover, while road surfaces were generally considered smooth enough for operation at up to the 30 mph legal maximum.

The lack of dampers was less acceptable in the provinces and I recall a hair-raising ride in one of the West Riding RT-type buses over sharply undulating road surfaces in an area prone to subsidence caused by coal mining. The driver put his foot down and the bus reached a particularly bad stretch at about 45 mph whereupon it began to pitch violently and I had visions of it going out of control.

Deliveries of complete RT-type buses to London Transport slowly gained momentum during the remainder of 1947, though it was September before the number in service passed the 50 mark. By the end of the year 171 were licensed for service. At this point, the title of the undertaking became the London Transport Executive, and a year later, at the end of 1948, the post-war RT fleet had grown to 900. By the end of 1949 it had become 1,639 and during 1950 a remarkable 1,126 had been added to bring the total to 2,765, making the RT the most numerous type in London service, a position it was to hold until the early 'seventies.

The increase in output was mainly due to Park Royal and Weymann both getting into their stride. It had always been intended that the former's output of RT-type bodies would be the greater, and for example though the second half of the 1944 order for 1,000 RT chassis was split into two batches of 250 (O961945-1194) and (O9611331-1580) the Park Royal body order this time amounted to 310 compared to Weymann's 190. In the event, some of this and subsequent Park Royal batches of bodies were diverted on to Leyland-built chassis to RT specification and numbered in the RTL series (see Chapter Three of No. 9 in this series on *Leyland Titans 1945-84*), but Weymann continued with AEC-built chassis only, apart from a small number of exceptions at a later stage. Historically, Weymann had always been more associated with London Transport's country bus department than the central area and it was decided that supply of standard RT bodywork in green livery for country services would be Weymann's responsibility. For lengthy periods that factory's RT output was exclusively

Gradually, as production got under way, the RT became a more familiar sight. In this 1948 Trafalgar Square scene, Park Royal-bodied RT359, delivered in March that year, is seen on route 15 followed by ST631, a petrol-engined AEC Regent dating from 1931 (and to be withdrawn in 1949), an STL-class Regent with 7.7-litre engine of 1936 and, just visible, an STD-class Leyland PD1 of 1946.

By 1949-50, new RT-type buses were rolling into London Transport's fleet in huge numbers. Seven buses are seen (left) ready to set off for London from Saunders' works in Beaumaris, Anglesey, on a rainy day late in 1949, with the mountainous coastline of North Wales in the background. Saunders had built nearly 150 of its main batch of 250 bodies by then, the appearance closely resembling the original post-war RT standard. The leading bus, RT1298, on chassis O9613289, entered service in January 1950.

This similar line-up was posed about three months later outside Park Royal's premises in north-west London. Park Royal and Weymann had both progressed to the body design without the roof-mounted route number box in the latter part of 1948 (though all vehicles were still being fitted with only one all-purpose front blind). The vehicle nearest the camera, RT1679, on chassis O9613621, was the second to appear in the 'all-red' livery, **entering service in April 1950.**

green, beginning in July 1948 towards the intitial batch of 250 at RT597.

Further bodybuilding capacity came with the decision to order 250 bodies from Saunders for RT1152-1401 and 120 from Cravens for RT1402-1521. Cravens adapted its standard five-bay body, on to which the standard RT cab was grafted, but Saunders built what was outwardly an almost indistinguishable replica of the standard RT body. Deliveries began towards the end of 1948 continuing until 1950, decidedly late but helping to augment the big intake in 1949-50. In both cases, some of the early deliveries were on chassis dating from 1946-47.

Meanwhile AEC had begun output of its second thousand post-war RT chassis which were numbered in one batch, O9612701-3700, the largest single batch to be given an unbroken run of numbers, though fleet numbers were, as usual, by no means in sequence. Delivery of these chassis began in January 1949 and was completed by May 1950. Yet a further

series of 370 numbered O9613749-4118 overlapped, being built between February and July 1950, probably due to alternative combinations of makes of equipment. The air pressure system could be either by Clayton Dewandre or Westinghouse, the individual items differing considerably in design, although functioning in the same way.

Body and chassis building was now much better matched and most of these chassis were soon bodied and in service, in some cases within a month or so of leaving Southall. As an example, O9612704 was put on the road from Muswell Hill garage as RT1108 in February 1949.

Although very standardised, the RT buses were the subject of numerous experiments, in some cases when new or recently in service. Despite the modest noise level of the standard version, six buses operating from Turnham Green garage (which was quite near Chiswick and hence the home of many buses involved in experiments) were fitted with Atlas

pilot injection in 1948 and I recall seeking them on the road and being impressed with the even quieter running, though individual examples varied. Fuel economy was worsened somewhat and the idea was not pursued.

More significantly, several buses received experimental Miller gearboxes which paved the way to the system eliminating the gear-change pedal and ultimately to fully-automatic control as offered on later models.

From 1947, RT-type chassis were generally regarded by AEC as being exclusive to London Transport, but when R. Edgley Cox was appointed General Manager of the St. Helens municipal transport system, he decided to order complete RT-type buses, doubtless recalling his early days with the LPTB. Both the chassis and Park Royal bodywork of fifteen buses supplied in 1950 and 25 more dating from 1952 conformed to the London specification in almost every respect.

(Above) Cravens Railway Carriage & Wagon Co Ltd based the 120 bodies it built for London Transport on its standard five-bay design of the time (see page 35) but with RT-design features grafted on — most obviously the cab, of which the waistline did not match the slightly lower level of that on the rest of the lower saloon. RT1442, seen here, was based on chassis O961289 and entered service in June 1949.

(Top right) Weymann's contribution to the total of standard RT bodywork included that on all but 20 of the green-painted vehicles of this type supplied for use by London Transport's country bus department, operating in the area later covered by London Country Bus Services Ltd. The steep hill out of High Wycombe is seen being climbed by RT3190 on a route which will take it past its home at Amersham garage, not long after it entered service in June 1950. It was based on chassis O9613693, one of the last of the one thousand chassis run (O9612701-3700) constituting the largest unbroken Regent batch of all, and including most of the London buses illustrated on this pair of pages.

The Green Line RT differed no more than cosmetically from the standard Weymann country-area product, with pale green stripe instead of cream and a bulls-eye motif on the upper deck, but the level of comfort was sufficient to make the term 'coach' always applied to Green Line vehicles acceptable — no advertising was carried. RT3259 was the last of 36 vehicles allocated to Romford garage in August 1950 for the busy routes operated into Aldgate, in those days also a trolleybus terminus. By that date, chassis production had moved on to a further batch and this vehicle was O9614086, though there were plenty more still to come, as described in Chapter Five.

After 1947, it was thought that the RT was exclusively a London model, but St. Helens Corporation caused some surprise by choosing what was virtually the current standard RT specification for both chassis and Park Royal bodywork on fifteen Regent III models. Number 60 (BDJ 60), on chassis 09615601, posed by the main-line railway embankment at Southall, was one of the first four delivered in June 1950. The livery, with a London-like red married to a much greater area of cream, suited the design well, but rather unimaginative use of the destination blinds was to spoil the end result somewhat.

The first Regent III chassis for Sydney is seen here being unloaded at the dockside early in 1947. The Department of Government Transport of New South Wales, responsible for running bus services in the Sydney area and already a big user of British double-deck chassis, placed an initial post-war order for fifteen chassis, numbered O961551-565, the first numbers to be allocated to export Regent III models. It seems quite possible, as explained in the previous chapter, that these were also originally intended to be the first Regent III chassis not built to the London Transport specification. The first of the chassis in this batch was built in December 1946, in the event not quite so early as the first home-market 'provincial' example, but an indication of the degree to which these Australian deliveries were pioneer vehicles is given by the engine numbers, all but one drawn from the first 39 examples of the A208 series of 9.6-litre engine introduced for the right-hand Mark III passenger models of non-RT design. The Sydney vehicles were of the 17ft. 6in. wheelbase standard for export models.

Chapter three:
The 'provincial' Regent III

The wartime and immediate post-war publicity led most observers to think that the Regent III as sold generally would be very like the RT-type in appearance and specification, apart from optional features and minor details, in much the same way that 7.7-litre O661-type Regents for provincial customers and London Transport were substantially similar in the late 'thirties. In particular, there had been direct reference to "greatly improved road visibility" in wartime advertisements for the forthcoming Regent III. Certainly, three other manufacturers - in those days completely independent - decided that

the RT's low bonnet line was a trend-setting feature, and Bristol, Crossley and Guy all introduced similarly low versions for their post-war bus chassis.

So the introduction of a quite different front-end design, with a taller radiator, for what was sometimes labelled the Regent Mark III Series 2 came as quite a surprise. There were at least two reasons behind this. One was the decision to fit an oil-bath air cleaner on the top of the engine, to give better protection against wear caused by operation in dust-laden atmosphere, especially in some overseas markets. Exports were greatly in mind and AEC's left-hand drive

models, unlike others, had a 'left-hand' engine, with all items likely to need regular attention accessible from the side remote from the driver. To minimise the number of special parts, as many as possible were simply turned round and thus the air cleaner, mounted towards the rear of the engine on right-hand models, was nearer the front on early left-hand types. As the engine was inclined to suit the transmission line, this made it slightly higher still, as well as nearer the radiator. Adequate radiator area for cooling in adverse conditions may also have been a factor.

There was also the bodybuilder's expectation that the chassis should have the lower half of the cab in position on arrival. This was the accepted policy, though London Transport, with both RT and STL, and Leyland's own-make bodywork, had shown that a neater end-result could be obtained from designing and building the entire cab as part of the body.

There was also undoubtedly an element of personal taste. The RT radiator's wire mesh grille and the exposed front dumb irons were reminiscent of pre-war practice on standard AEC models and the visible part of the radiator surround, slimmer on the cab side than the remainder to suit the almost flush-fitting cab front was perhaps slightly odd-looking,

The combination of chromium-plated radiator shell with vertically slatted grille had previously been seen on the Regal Mark III (model O862) single-decker introduced in 1935. There was even a hint of the style of front mudguard to be favoured for the Regent III. The wet-liner engine used in this model was a precursor of the AV470 unit used in the medium-weight Regent V, as described in Chapter Seven.

On the face of things, chassis numbered O961629-638 do not seem likely candidates for being pioneers in a system where new models were supposed to begin at '001. However, Sheffield's batch of ten chassis with these numbers were the first provincial Regent III models to enter service. This was partly because of Weymann's capabilities of building bodywork more quickly than most concerns at that time, but in fact the chassis were among the earliest of the type to be completed — one of the batch received A208 engine number 5 — and even in numerical terms this may well have originally been intended to be the first home-market batch of 'Series 2' chassis (model type number O961/2); the only earlier-numbered chassis being the total of eleven included in the mainly RT series with numbers up to O961188. Sheffield Corporation's No. 532 (JWB 732) on chassis O961634 is seen at Southall on a wintry-looking day before delivery in time to enter service in March 1947. The Weymann body design suited this version of the chassis particularly well, the use of four-bay layout nodding to the RT concept but the rest being characteristic of this builder's elegant designs of the early post-war period.

considered on its own. What emerged for the Series 2 version had quite strong echoes of the Regal Mark II (model O682) of 1935-39, the slightly lighter-than-standard single-decker with the so-called 6.6-litre six-cylinder oil engine then offered alongside the standard Regal. The mudguard treatment and use of a chromium-plated radiator shell with vertical slats was almost directly repeated, save that the radiator was deeper, and much the same proportions as on standard Regents and Regals from 1938.

There seems little doubt that this was John Rackham's idea of what a half-cab bus should look like - neat and stylish if just a shade conservative, as perhaps might be expected from someone then in his 'sixties. It is interesting that Leyland and AEC had come up with not dissimilar concepts, save that AEC preferred the deep radiator that had been considered modern-looking in the late 'thirties but was perhaps now more traditional than Leyland's post-war choice of a wider shape. From the front, the general proportions were much as on previous standard 7.7-litre Regents - the height to the top of the radiator above the frame was virtually identical - but the slightly more pronounced upward slope along the bonnet top to clear the air cleaner pushed the minimal bulkhead window level up. So the "greatly improved road visibility" which could fairly be claimed for the RT certainly didn't apply to lower-deck passengers in a provincial Regent III.

The author, as a youthful bus enthusiast, was bitterly disappointed in this and, nearly forty years on, still thinks it was a pity, particularly as Leyland later showed how quite a large

air cleaner could fit under the RT-type bonnet. The Series 2 front-end was also less compact than the RT version with a bonnet length of 4ft. 9 5/16in., nearly 3in. more than the RT.

However, there were numerous other differences between the 'plain' O961 model, which signified the RT-type chassis, and the O961/2, which was the designation applied to the provincial Regent III Series 2 model in 1946/47. The latter's frame was of full-length type, the side-members continuing under the rear platform rather than ending just after the body mounting points at the rear end of the rear springs, as on the post-war RT. The springs were different, generally giving a softer ride, with shock absorbers to damp out undue rebound oscillation. AEC's patent stabiliser was fitted to limit the amount of roll permitted beyond a pre-set degree. Larger front tyres were used, with a different axle.

The dynamo was mounted on the engine, being accommodated by a characteristic bulge on the bonnet side, an idea first seen on a non-standard Regent of 1939-40 (see page 75 of No. 7 of this series). The bonnet top itself, deeper than usual, used a simple yet ingenious over-centre spring principle, allowing it to be opened by a firm upward push on a knob at the front corner and being then held open by the same spring until pulled down, simplifying access for minor servicing.

These and numerous other small differences, such as the style of pedals, meant that remarkably few complete units were common between the RT and provincial versions - the engine on the latter of was type A208 instead of A204, for example. Yet under the skin there was a great deal in common,

with most major components sharing basically the same pressings, castings and forgings. The economics of manufacture would doubtless have been improved if the designs had been more nearly identical but were much better than in later years when AEC buses for London and elsewhere became almost completely divorced.

Both versions were popular with drivers, passengers and, with a few reservations, operators' engineering staff. If the engine was set to the maximum output of 125 bhp at 1800 rpm instead of the economy 110 or 115 bhp settings, the available performance was just about unrivalled. At that date, only Leyland's new 9.8-litre PD2 model could equal this engine output among double-deckers and it was much easier to get the power on to the road through AEC's air-operated preselective gearbox, with its light-acting controls, than Leyland's synchromesh unit, with inevitably fairly heavy lever and clutch pedal movement. Admittedly, it was also quite easy to give passengers a jerky ride, unless reasonable care was taken, but the preselector gearbox was robust and reliable. The air pressure system now generally worked well, again with a reduction of driver effort, and revisions in design made the brakes better able to stand up to the hard use they were liable to get.

AEC's sales campaign based on the theme that the Regent III was a superior sort of bus struck a responsive chord after the years of wartime austerity. The demand for new vehicles was such that no serious builder of double-deckers was likely to have any difficulty in selling them, but the specification - more elaborate than

The first Series 2 versions of the Regent III chassis were built for the Scottish Motor Traction Co Ltd, one — in all probability O961010, which incidentally had A208 engine number 1 — being used for a well-publicised combined demonstration run to Glasgow in November 1946. However, the batch of chassis involved, O961010-018, were not bodied immediately, being combined with later batches to allow 40 similar buses to be bodied by Alexander, in those days an SMT subsidiary, and placed in service between December 1947 and March 1948. The 53-seat lowbridge body design was almost identical to that being applied by Alexander to Leyland PD1 chassis for its own fleet and very similar to Alexander's 'Leyland-like' wartime design. When first seen around 1943 this had seemed better looking than most of its utility contemporaries but by 1948 seemed very austere, especially for the 'glamorous' Regent III. The vehicle seen here is BB38 (FFS 159), on chassis

O961834, new in February 1948 and one of the last to remain in service, not being withdrawn until 1969.

Another Regent III with a very early number was ordered at about the same time as the initial SMT batch by the Ebor Bus Co Ltd of Mansfield, being given the chassis number O961018. Ebor also had two other chassis included in the same order, O961188 and O9611322, all three receiving Brush metal-framed bodywork of a type produced on 34 Regents for Leicester City Transport and the Ebor order went through the Brush works at the same time, the Ebor vehicles in question being delivered in November 1948. However, O961018 was transferred to another nearby independent operator, E. Naylor & Sons of South Normanton, being registered MRB 709, as shown here, ultimately passing to the Trent fleet in 1956.

any of its competitors - was accepted quite widely. Naturally enough, previous regular customers for Regents with fluid flywheels and preselective gearboxes like Sheffield, Leeds and Bradford, took to the new model but others previously favouring crash gearbox versions, such as some of the BET companies, or in several cases not

AEC customers at all, like West Riding, adopted it, sometimes with great enthusiasm.

Deliveries of Regent III Series 2 chassis began by November 1946, one of the first being used for a combined publicity and delivery run to the AEC depot in Glasgow that month. It was for the Scottish Motor Traction Co Ltd

fleet and may well have been one of the O961010-017 batch which were the lowest numbered O961/2 models, having been among the earliest Regent III models for which the sales orders were issued. Evidently SMT preferred to take the Series 2 rather than RT-type chassis, similar remarks applying to the two chassis allocated to Ebor of Mansfield, O961018 and O961188, and one for Central SMT, O961019.

In the event, none of these were among the earliest O961/2 models to enter service as complete vehicles, as that distinction seems to belong to ten vehicles supplied to Sheffield Corporation in March 1947, on chassis O961639-648, though within the following three or four months several other operators had examples in service. The Sheffield buses had a

The first of the Sydney Regent III buses, chassis number O961551, which had A208 engine number 2, was duly bodied to typically Australian style by Commonwealth Engineering, entering service as number 792 in 1947 and followed by 30 more similar buses before the end of the year. The initial order for fifteen chassis had been followed by one for 35 and then in the period between November 1947 and September 1948 some 242 more of the 17ft. 6in.-wheelbase chassis were shipped, numbered 9612E2094-2335.

Roe was among the earliest bodybuilders of the provincial-type Regent III. Soon after the initial batch of fifteen for Leeds, delivered in April-May 1947, came six with basically similar 56-seat bodywork for Sunderland Corporation, a regular Roe customer since 1930 but not previously one for AEC chassis. Number 85 (GR 9116) on chassis O961853, is seen here just before delivery, resplendent in the red and cream livery still current at that date. Sunderland thereafter reverted to its preference for Gardner-engined buses, mainly Daimler or Guy, no further AECs being purchased until some Reliance single-deckers arrived in 1960.

West Monmouthshire Omnibus Board was the rather grand title chosen for the joint undertaking set up by two urban district councils, Bedwellty and Mynydislwyn, to run buses in their part of the famous valleys, then employing thousands of men in the coal mines. Double-deck bus operation had begun during the war years, and one Regent III was placed in service in 1948, No. 17 (GWO 522) on chassis O961884. Massey Bros' standard lowbridge body design of the period had an unusually strong sweep-back at the front of the upper deck, as seen here. Two more preselective Regent models with 53-seat bodywork, but this time by the Cardiff concern, Bruce Coach Works, were purchased in 1949.

Another market for the 17ft. 6in.-wheelbase export model was Ireland, the Great Northern Railway having been an AEC customer since 1937. Ten vehicles added to the fleet in 1948 had five-bay bodywork based on Park Royal metal framework but assembled and completed in the GNR workshops. Number 289 (IY 5391) on chassis O9611694 is seen here in the smart Oxford blue livery in O'Connell Street, Dublin. These, plus seven more on slightly later chassis completed at about the same time, passed to Coras Iompair Eireann in 1959 with the rest of the GNR fleet, joining the Regent III already in the CIE fleet, Leyland-dominated though it was.

Several bodybuilders produced 'special' four-bay bodywork for the Regent III, quite often confining it to this chassis model. Park Royal's interpretation was this metal-framed design, a distinctive blend of curves and some rather angular detailing. The first examples appeared in the latter part of 1947, including eleven for the Huddersfield Corporation and LMS Railway Joint Omnibus Committee of which No. 152 (DCX 952) on chassis O961892 is seen here, this being a Corporation rather than railway-owned bus. It was not built in large numbers, being favoured by three traditonal AEC and Park Royal customers — Huddersfield, Morecambe and West Bridgford.

A tradition of Commercial Motor Show exhibits bodied by Roe on AEC Regent chassis for the Leeds municipal fleet had begun in 1935 and the October 1948 example was No. 600 (MNW 600), an early example of the home-market 8ft.-wide version of the Regent III, which accompanied a left-hand drive Regal III chassis as the passenger exhibits on AEC's own stand. The body design was a development of the 'Leeds City Pullman' four-bay style first seen on the corresponding 1937 exhibit and virtually repeated on a vehicle built for the 1939 Show, cancelled due to the war, these being respectively numbered 400 and 500 in the Leeds fleet. Such designs were still being regarded as 'Show specials', Roe's normal production being the five-bay design shown on the previous page. The chassis number was 9612E2355, the model number prefix being in accordance with the new system introduced at the beginning of 1948.

Another bodybuilder to produce a four-bay body for the Regent III was Charles Roberts Ltd of Wakefield, primarily a railway rolling stock manufacturer but then making one of its intermittent ventures into the bus bodybuilding business. Orders for 25 vehicles for Sheffield, all built in 1948, doubtless led to an inspection of one of the Weymann-bodied Regents as shown on page 27 but Roberts' designers evolved their own interpretation, as shown by No. 122 (LWA 22), on chassis O9611665. It was delivered in October 1948 but is seen here in June 1950, by which date the cream paint on the part of the cab front above the radiator had become blackened in a way apt to be characteristic of the provincial Regent III — it seemed that the fan created an air flow which would carry fragments of dirt through a gap behind the radiator shell. Note the Leyland Lion dating from 1932 then in use as a canteen.

four-bay version of what was otherwise largely the standard Weymann body of the period, soon to become a familiar sight on this chassis for municipal and company fleets and remaining among the most successful visually, with its flowing lines and outswept skirt panels.

The idea that the Regent III deserved something special in terms of body design was not uncommon and the author detects the influence of AEC's effective publicity and possibly of John Rackham himself in this. Several other builders produced designs which were at least initially exclusive to the Regent III. Park Royal, at that stage not financially associated with AEC, produced a metal-framed design used by Huddersfield and West Bridgford although the first examples, delivered in the late summer of 1947, using basically the same structure were Birmingham's fifteen on RT-type chassis with appearance radically altered by their inclined windscreen. All of these were of four-bay style and hence doubtless inspired by the London RT body design, though Park Royal did not adopt other RT features into its own styles until the early 'fifties. Other four-bay 'specials' for the Regent III included one by Roberts, initially for Sheffield, in 1948 and Roe's 1948 Show vehicle for Leeds, though this revived a tradition going back to the 1937 Show and pre-dating even the original RT.

Despite the flood of orders for the standard Regent III, there was a core of resistance among some AEC users which still favoured something nearer the Regent II specification, to varying degrees. City of Oxford Motor Services Ltd had long disliked fluid transmission, being one of the few

major operators to receive a batch of vehicles so equipped in the early days (in this case six Regents in 1932) which did not subsequently standardise on the type, either wholly or to some degree. AEC vehicles had been chosen almost exclusively from 1930, including three batches of Regent II models in 1946-48. An order for fourteen Regent III delivered towards the end of 1948 broke new ground in combining the 9.6-litre engine with the traditional AEC D124 crash gearbox and vacuum brakes.

The combination produced what amounted to a new model, for numerous related changes were

involved, starting with the frame, for although of Regent III type, it had a completely different flexible engine mounting system, not seen on any previous AEC model, to suit the combination of the 9.6-litre engine with clutch and gearbox directly behind it. The system of two rubber rings, one high up at the front of the engine and a larger one behind the flywheel as used on the RT and fluid transmission O961/2, could not be used, partly because the gearbox was where the rear ring would be and partly because it was not suitable for the torque reaction created when the clutch was engaged. So a more conventional system using

East Lancashire Coachbuilders Ltd had initially supplied four-bay bodywork to Eastbourne on Leyland PD1 chassis in 1946, so here any association with AEC chassis was no more than the general interest aroused by the RT, etc. However, four Regent III models placed in service in the autumn of 1948 had basically similar bodywork by Bruce, East Lancs' Cardiff-based associate. Number 30 (JK 9987) is seen here on the occasion of a visit to Eastbourne by the Southern Counties Touring Society. Its chassis number was O9612639, one of the highest O961-prefix numbers issued to a provincial Regent III.

The first Regent III chassis combining the 9.6-litre engine and the traditional AEC crash gearbox were built for City of Oxford Motor Services Ltd, entering service in 1948, this combination immediately becoming standard in this fleet, remaining so until the introduction of the synchromesh gearbox version as described in Chapter Five. The example shown here was one of ten which entered service in 1950 and having Park Royal 52-seat lowbridge bodywork, the latter being of a style not unlike the version supplied to Reading on Regent II chassis. Number 156 (OFC 380) was on chassis 9612A4682, this batch also being of interest because of the A213-type engine fitted. This was basically as the A208 but with sump modified to suit the provision of a stabiliser on the front axle, optional at the time – quite a number of vehicles were so equipped, though when the front stabiliser became standard the production engine was modified to suit. Note the Oxford fleet's solitary Bristol K5G, allocated in wartime, visible on the left.

three rubber blocks, the rear two widely spaced, one each side of the flywheel, was adopted.

The remaining units were a combination of Regent III and virtually Regent II items, the end result being at first identified within AEC's drawing office as "O961/2 to SV179", the latter being the number of the relevant 'Standard Variation' list covering optional features.

Meanwhile, a further step in the same direction was the fitting of the A173 7.7-litre engine and the same D124 gearbox, again with vacuum brakes, into the Regent III chassis. There was particular interest in this combination for the equivalent single-deck Regal III but a Regent III 7.7-litre prototype

chassis was produced, being given a chassis number U129796, in the vast U-number series mainly used for freshly-designed or experimental parts before being put into production. This model was to be type O681, thus avoiding any break with the 9.6-litre implication associated with O961.

At this point it was decided to introduce a variation in the chassis type number system to cover the complexities that had arisen. The basic three-figure model codes remained unchanged but, in general, the 'O' prefix was dropped as its original significance in identifying oil-engined chassis was no longer needed, no petrol models having been offered since 1939. Instead, the series number

became part of the code as the fourth figure and a letter added to signify the type of gearbox on passenger models. Thus the standard O961/2 became 9612E and the crash gearbox equivalent became 9612A, the A standing for 'AEC', somewhat illogically. Similarly, the O681 chassis became 6811A, this version not having yet progressed beyond its first 'series'. The new system was introduced with effect from 1st January 1948 and applied to chassis numbers of chassis being produced from then onwards. The only passenger model to continue unchanged was the 'plain' O961, which thus exclusively now referred to London Transport-type RT chassis.

As orders were by no means built in

The concept of what were, in effect, Regent II mechnical units in a Regent III chassis and having the latter's appearance was carried to its logical conclusion with the introduction of a 7.7-litre crash gearbox version of the model. By the time it went into production its designation had become 6811A under the new system introduced in 1948. Liverpool Corporation was the first and largest customer and, on the right of this view, A394 (HKF 870) is one of the 75 vehicles in question, on chassis 6811A045. They received bodywork based on Weymann shells but to a rather austere Liverpool specification and completed in the Corporation's workshops. Its neighbour on the steam cleaning ramps is A761 (MKB 954), an 8ft.-wide bus from a later batch of 50 chassis of type 9613A, with 9.6-litre engines, crash gearboxes and Crossley bodywork dating from 1951 – note the rubber-edged mudguards, a distinctive Liverpool feature.

The BET group as a whole was interested in the crash-gearbox version of the 9.6-litre Regent — indeed had this not been so, the option might not have been introduced. Among BET subsidiaries which took early examples of the 9612A model was Western Welsh, for whom twelve were built and fitted with Brush 56-seat bodywork in the autumn of 1948. Brush Coachworks Ltd had been one of the biggest suppliers to BET companies but this association was fading and this style of bodywork, visually different to the Leicester version shown on page 28, was quite rare. Number 622 (DKG 622), on chassis 9612A4146, is seen in Cardiff.

A minority of BET companies continued with the preselective-gearbox version of the Regent III for a year or two after the crash gearbox option was introduced. Among them was Devon General, whose 1949 delivery consisted of 26 of the 9612E model. Seen here is DR569 (KOD 569) on chassis 9612E2479, in spotless condition and complete with RT-style rear wheel discs to provide the finishing touch to the Weymann bodywork, on which the traditional outswept skirt had been specified. Most of the batch operated in the Exeter area in their early years, later being transferred to Torquay.

the same sequence as the numbers reserved for them, the new-style designations began to appear over quite a wide range of 961-series chassis numbers. For example, Hull Corporation ordered 50 chassis of which the first 24 were delivered in 1947 as O961669-692 but the balance of 26 appeared as 9612E693-718 when placed in service in the early months of 1949. These were the lowest-numbered 9612E variants and, at the other extreme, Eastbourne Corporation took delivery of 'provincial' Regent III models 09612637-2640 in 1948, an indication in itself of the volume of orders that had flowed into AEC before the end of 1947.

The initial Oxford crash-gearbox order itself acted as another illustration. It materialised as O9611739-1743 and 9612A1744-1752, the last of the batch being shown with Northern Coachbuilders body on that bodybuilder's stand at the 1948 Commercial Motor Show. It was, in fact, more general interest from the BET group of companies to which Oxford belonged that lay behind the development of the 9612A. In 1949 another group company which had thus far taken only Regent II double-deckers since the war period, South Wales Transport Co Ltd, took 30 of the 9612A type. Yet it is significant that two other BET companies, Devon General and Rhondda, had continued ordering 9612E models after starting the post-war period with RT-type chassis, though 1949 was the final year

in both cases, and Hebble also favoured the 9612E up to 1950.

Meanwhile, Liverpool Corporation had placed the first and largest order for the 7.7-litre version, 75 vehicles numbered 6811A001-075, placed in service in 1948-49 along with 25 of the 9.6-litre fluid transmission type. Although Liverpool also bought the prototype 7.7-litre chassis mentioned above, the next batch of 100 Regent III for this city were of the 9612E type, entering service between December 1949 and August 1951. The 6811A could hardly be classed as a great success

The Tilling group of companies did not 'voluntarily' buy any Regent III buses due to its policy of standardisation on Bristol chassis, but nationalisation of both of them and the SMT group of companies in 1948-49 led to the diversion of an order for six of the 7.7-litre 6811A models with 53-seat lowbridge Northern Counties bodywork from Western SMT to the Hants & Dorset company, then taking AEC-engined Bristol chassis for much of its fleet additions. Western was at the time in process of taking delivery of what were originally to be 70 Regent III 9.6-litre preselective models with similar bodywork, of which the first had entered service in July 1947; delivery continued until June 1950 by which time 58 had been supplied, the remaining twelve being cancelled. Hants & Dorset's JEL 756 on chassis 6811A081 entered service in June 1949.

when considered individually, for only 22 other examples were built up to 1950 though several hundred of the equivalent single-decker had been supplied, mainly to company fleets and independent operators, so the design was justified on that score.

Interest in the 9612A was also limited at first, with BET group companies as the main users, though the volume and the number of individual concerns involved steadily grew. Noteworthy among other early users was St. Helens Corporation, which took eight of this model in 1949

before the change of policy to complete RT-type buses mentioned in the last chapter. However, gradually, as increasing operating costs mainly due to wage increases began to cause operators to look for means of making savings, fuel economy again began to be regarded as important. A preselective Regent III, driven hard, as was not difficult, certainly used more fuel than some, though not all, of its competitors. On the other hand, the possible saving directly attributable to the transmission was rarely more than about 1 mpg and fuel costs as a whole were of diminishing importance, though this was by no means generally realised at the time.

Good standards of vehicle reliability were taken for granted although London Transport had found, even in the mid-'thirties, that fluid transmission cut repair costs and eliminated the need for frequent attention to both clutch and conventional gearboxes in city operation. Elsewhere conditions were yet to become sufficiently severe for this to be accepted outside what might be called the traditional users of epicyclic-gearbox buses - indeed, even some of them began to waver -

Newcastle's final batch of Regent III models consisted of 40 9612A-type, placed in service in the latter half of 1950, although this was one of the first such instances.

By this date, 961-series chassis numbers had reached over 5000 and while some of these were reserved for vehicles yet to be delivered and others had been, or were to be, cancelled before being built, the majority were in service, about half being London RT-type buses.

Sales order documents relating to export vehicles had begun to be issued even before those relating to the first post-war RT-type chassis. The standard export version of the O961/2, later 9612E, had a 17ft. 6in. wheelbase and 8ft. width and the first batch of fifteen for Sydney, O961550-565, left Southall between December 1946 and March 1947, to be followed by further batches, including one of 242 vehicles mostly shipped in 1948. Some overseas operators favoured the home-market 16ft. 4in. wheelbase, including Pretoria, Germiston, East London and Durban in South Africa, all of which took batches built in 1947. On the other hand, the Great Northern Railway in Eire, a Regent customer since the

'thirties, favoured the 17ft. 6in. version for ten buses with Park Royal body shells assembled by GNR in 1948.

The first home-market 8ft.-wide Regents were seven with East Lancashire bodywork supplied to Rochdale Corporation in August 1948 (O961872-878), that undertaking benefitting from the favourable attitude to the operation of vehicles of this width evident at the time in the North Western Traffic Area. The 1948 Show exhibit for Leeds already mentioned was of this width but as a 'one-off' and 8ft.-wide Regents remained a rarity in Britain until the latter part of 1949, when SMT took 20 with Duple lowbridge bodywork and Nottingham placed 41 in service with Roberts bodies, followed by Cardiff early in 1950 with 20 with East Lancashire-design bodies, all 9612E models. The 40 Newcastle 9612A models of late 1950 were of this width as were 24 buses on the same chassis for Western Welsh delivered in the same period.

The addition of bodybuilding to the ACV group's activities as a result of the take-over of Crossley, Park Royal and Roe came too late to materially affect the Regent III era and in the 1947-50 period there was immense variety in the makes and styles of bodywork fitted. Among the more prominent of the 'new-comers' — though actually established in the 'thirties — was Northern Coachbuilders Ltd of Newcastle, who understandably chose a Regent in the smart livery of Sheffield Corporation as the subject of this advertising photograph. It was one of ten supplied towards the end of 1947. Number 582 (KWB 82) was based on chassis O9611652. Ten more followed in the next two years, 1949-50.

The Sheffield fleet was itself a scene of remarkable variety as body orders were spread around to try and obtain reasonably rapid delivery. Cravens, the local concern, did not come into the picture until 1949-50 and then only to the extent of fifteen 56-seat bodies on Regent III chassis — in the 'thirties, the firm had been one of Sheffield's two most important bodybuilders. However, Cravens was then still completing the 120 bodies on RT-type chassis for London Transport, the maximum number the firm had felt able to offer when enquiries were made for delivery in 1948. The first bodies of this basic design were built for Alexander early in 1948 on 25 Guy chassis. Compare this view of No. 246 (LWB 746) on chassis 9612E4299, with that of RT1442 on page 25.

Barnard Ltd, a Norwich-based bodybuilder, only figured briefly in the world of double-deck buses for municipal customers but secured orders for nineteen 56-seat highbridge bodies for Dundee Corporation, including nine on Regent III, in 1949-50. Number 140 (AYJ 370), 9612E4700, displays conservative but well-proportioned lines as it is seen posed outside the entrance to the AEC works in Windmill Lane, Southall This photograph also shows, in the background, the prominent AEC sign on what was always known locally as the Iron Bridge carrying the main Western Region railway line diagonally over the Uxbridge Road. A 'blue triangle' AEC badge is just hidden by the canopy of the bus, the wording thus reading "AEC Motor Vehicles, Head Office & Works" with a large arrow to direct traffic to turn into Windmill Lane.

NORTHERN COACHBUILDERS. LTD.

Another transferred order within the nationalised sector led to the creation of a new class of vehicles for London Transport, then in need of new lowbridge double-deckers. Midland General Omnibus Co Ltd, state-owned from 1948, had ordered its then standard combination of Regent III 9612E chassis and Weymann bodywork in 53-seat lowbridge form and though, ideally, LTE would have preferred a lowbridge version of the RT, it was agreed that the Midland General specification was acceptable with minor modifications. So MGO received only ten such vehicles, in March-April 1950, of which the first, No. 421 (ONU 630) on chassis 9612E4721 is seen above. London Transport received 20, beginning in May of the same year and numbered RLH1-20. The last, registered KYY 520 and on chassis 9612E5041, is seen above left on service 410 operated from Godstone garage. Unusually, LTE's destination display was less elaborate than the original and the only other noticeable external difference was the type of headlamps and sidelamps fitted.

Roe, having pioneered the 'modern' four-bay double-decker as long ago as 1937 with the first of a series of Show-model Regents for Leeds City Transport, finally put a similar design into volume production in the summer of 1949, when it was announced that 100 were to be built for the Leeds fleet. The first 25, with decidedly inappropriate MUG registration numbers for so strikingly effective a design, entered service in September of that year, but No. 464 (MUG 464) on chassis 9612E2370, seen here, had been completed in July. They were in the very restrained greyish-blue livery favoured by W. Vane Morland, shortly due to retire as the Leeds undertaking's General Manager. For some time other customers still received the five-bay version shown on page 29. In practice, there were 75 buses of the 7ft. 6in.-wide design shown, the total being made up by the 1948 Show vehicle and 24 on 9613E chassis (see Chapter Five).

At Newcastle, a batch of 40 Regent III delivered in the latter part of 1950 was notable in three respects. After choosing the preselective model for 61 earlier Regent III deliveries in 1947-49, these were 9612A models, with the crash gearbox. They were also 8ft.-wide and though the body contract went again to Northern Coachbuilders, as had been the case with the previous 30 vehicles, these were of a new design with strong resemblance to Eastern Coach Works practice, due to the apppointment at NCB of an ex-ECW General Manager, Bill Bramham. Financial problems led to the closure of NCB soon after this design appeared. Number 332 (NVK 332) on chassis 9612A5294 is seen here — No. 341 of the same period is preserved.

Looking very like a trolleybus, albeit an oddly-proportioned one with an ill-at-ease mixture of Birmingham City Transport and London Transport styling ideas, the solitary Regent IV poses for an official picture at the entrance to Southall works in the late summer of 1949. The legal owner lettering reads "AEC Ltd", these initials having become the official title of the manufacturing firm the previous year on the formation of the Associated Commercial Vehicles group. Note the nearside cab door, which was the only means of entry for the driver, a step ring being provided on the front wheel. The use of a rear-hinged door extending the full length of the cab was a revival of an idea, doubtless of Rackham origin, used on the AEC-designed bodywork on some early 16ft. 3in.-wheelbase Regents of 1931-32 — see page 36 of No. 7 of this series.

Chapter four:
Underfloor interlude, 1950

In 1948 there was much talk in the industry of underfloor engines and AEC was putting such words into deeds. It had produced a prototype single-decker of this layout aimed at the Canadian market in 1939 and, though the war had halted further action, the first Regal IV prototype was bodied in January 1949. This was also a single-decker, but built to the contemporary British length limit of 27ft. 6in. and by the time the official announcement about the range of similar models being offered for home and overseas use was made at the end of December, an underfloor-engined double-decker had been shown to operators with the idea of following up with a corresponding Regent IV.

The thought behind this development was that if single-deckers were going to switch to underfloor-engined layout, as indeed was largely confirmed so far as AEC's markets were concerned within a couple of years or so, the double-deckers should use similar components. This would have retained the use of largely common units between single- and double-deck chassis that had been characteristic of Rackham's designs not only going back to the original Regal and Regent of 1929 but also established in the first Leyland Tiger and Titan models of 1927.

John Rackham, now nearing retirement, had been through this process of introducing an unfamiliar vehicle layout to the somewhat conservative British operating industry before, with the side-engined AEC Q-type from 1932. In that case, he saw the double-decker as the version gaining most benefit from the layout, with the entrance ahead of the front axle, in the manner to become familiar on the Leyland Atlantean over a quarter of the century later. In the Q, the staircase to the upper-deck was over the offside front wheel and the engine immediately behind it. Operators were not convinced, however, and only 23 examples of the Q double-decker (plus one six-wheel Green Line version) were built, such modest success as the model achieved being concentrated on the single-deck version, as explained more fully in No. 2 of this series of volumes.

It may be that this chastening experience deterred the use of the front-entrance layout on the Regent IV. There had been a fair degree of interest in double-deckers on conventional front-engined chassis with the entrance immediately behind the nearside front bulkhead in the mid-'thirties, but even this had died away almost completely in the post-war period. AEC had not sold any such

vehicles since about 1938 and two independent operators, Barton Transport of Chilwell, Nottingham, and Birch Bros of Kentish Town, London, had been the only users of the layout since 1946, in both cases on Leyland PD1 chassis.

So it was decided to design the Regent IV for rear-entrance bodywork. There was to be minimum front overhang, the driving position being directly over the front axle as on a conventional double-decker. The layout was otherwise very like the Regal IV model 9821E, with the A219 engine, virtually a standard 9.6-litre unit laid on its side with re-arranged lubrication and fuel injection systems, mounted under the frame fairly close behind the front axle. The model number, had it been put into production, would doubtless have been 9811E, as the chassis had the usual air-operated epicyclic gearbox and brake system.

It was sent to Crossley Motors Ltd, which had been taken over the previous year, for bodying. The completed vehicle had a most curious appearance, basically like a trolleybus but with its proportions somewhat distorted and an odd mixture of styles. The curved profile at the front was possibly inspired by the RT but had an exaggerated rake towards the top. The front corner pillars were very thick, Birmingham-style, and the continuous metal louvres over the windows ended abruptly also in the manner then standard on that city's buses. Crossley had body contracts in hand for the Birmingham undertaking and was involved in the development of its 'new look' buses at the time, as mentioned in Chapter Six.

The body could be described as of four-and-a-half bay style, with the 'half' bay on each side at the rear, and glazed rather than 'blind' as on the slightly shorter RT equivalent. Perhaps most oddly of all, on the upper-deck there was a full-length opening window above the half-bay, with a very short shaped window at the rear. Within, the RT influence was much more evident, even extending to the lower-deck ceiling contour - the seats, and even the moquette, were to London Transport pattern.

In practical terms, the design had little to offer as compared to a conventional double-decker of the time. The seating capacity of the Crossley body was 30 up and 30 down, making a total of 60, which had been achieved on several batches of standard Regents for various operators from 1932 onwards. The absence of the conventional bonnet allowed the cab to be reduced in length by perhaps 9in., making it possible to squeeze in an extra row of forward-facing seats,

though the spacing had to be reduced to do so. The driver's cab was doubtless quieter and a noteworthy detail was that entry was from the kerb side.

The vehicle visited various operators, including Brighton and Nottingham, during the winter of 1949-50 but does not seem to have produced much enthusiasm. It is said that the unladen weight was excessive. It was evidently decided to have another attempt at arriving at a satisfactory body design and this time the work was entrusted to Park Royal. The bus re-emerged in June 1950, this time in Leeds City Transport livery and legal lettering, improved considerably in appearance and with seating capacity increased to 64, with an extra row of seats on the top deck. The single-skin roof may have been adopted to help in meeting tilt-test requirements with these extra seats. The four-and-a-half bay lower deck layout was retained and this leads one to wonder whether any of the original body was retained. Careful examination of photographs indicates that the Park Royal body was completely new in terms of structure and panels, though the seating, most of the opening windows and some other fittings may have been retained. It bore the fleet number 800, which strongly suggests that it was planned to display it at the 1950 Commercial Motor Show, as Leeds fleet numbers

200, 400, 500 and 600 had all been used on AEC buses built for previous Shows and 700 was to be a Regent III which did appear at the 1950 Show, as indicated in the next chapter.

But not only did No. 800 not appear at the Show, it seems never even to have gone out on a demonstration tour. It was evidently decided that the whole project had little chance of being a commercial success and the Regent IV was dropped even before being officially announced. The vehicle is believed to have been scrapped almost immediately.

One cannot help but speculate as to what might have happened if a more courageous line had been adopted and the front entrance, already seen as logical for the underfloor-engined single-decker, had been standardised for the double-decker. Would the operating industry have rejected it, as with the Q, or would AEC have tapped the market ultimately fulfilled by the Leyland Atlantean and Daimler Fleetline a decade later? The engine installation was neatly done, the lower saloon floor being raised slightly on the right hand side under the first four rows of seats but the gangway kept clear, an achievement which could have led to a vehicle on the lines of the Midland Red D10, the Volvo Citybus and the latest generation Leyland Lion.

The Regent IV chassis seen outside the experimental department at Southall works. Except for the front-end the chassis layout quite closely resembled that of the single-decker Regal IV, with A219 horizontal 9.6-litre engine, preselective gearbox and underslung worm-drive rear axle in much the same relative positions. The frame level was lowered somewhat, except directly over the engine, and at the front end the driving position was directly over the front axle in almost the standard Regent III location. Note the gantry partly visible in the background on the left of the picture, used for mounting cast-iron test loads on both experimental and other chassis.

Part of the lifeguard rail lifted with the side panel to give access to the engine. This view also shows the lack of a cab door on this side, with full-depth sliding window to permit signalling; semaphore-type indicators were also provided.

This upper-deck view shows the strong RT body 'flavour' within, though the thick Birmingham-style front corner pillars seem out of place.

A slightly different livery had been adopted by the time the vehicle was sent out for examination by operators, the shaping of the between-decks panel at the rear resembling that over the platform on the opposite side and adding to the 'odd' effect of the pillar spacing. It had not been registered and is seen here in Nottingham in September 1949, bearing AEC trade plates 368 H — these would have allowed demonstration runs but not operation in public service. Operators do not seem to have been very impressed, since the 60-seat capacity could be matched on a conventional double-decker and it may have been this that prompted the decision to let Park Royal have a go at an improved body design.

The contrast between the RT-style lower-deck, especially in the area of the ceiling, of the original Crossley body on the Regent IV (top left) and the more orthodox Park Royal version (centre left) is readily apparent. The Park Royal body was completed in Leeds City Transport's newly-adopted two-tone green livery in June 1950 and the fleet number 800 indicates that it was intended to exhibit the vehicle at the Earls Court Show the following autumn. Seating capacity was now 64, with 34 on top, and appearance much improved. But the whole project was dropped and the vehicle soon dismantled. Even so, the seating layout and general proportions of the body may well have influenced the Routemaster, which began with an underfloor radiator despite its front-mounted engine.

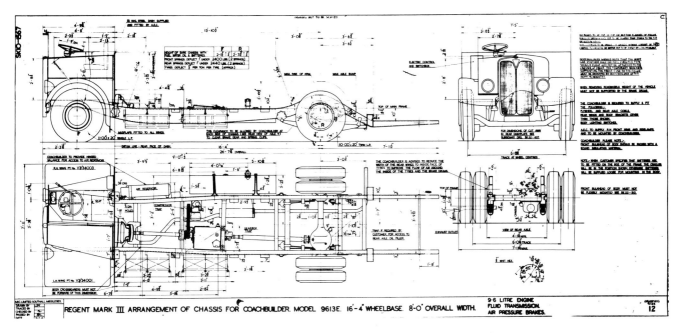

AEC LIMITED SOUTHALL MIDDLESEX
DRAWN BY
TRACED BY
CHECKED BY
DATE

REGENT MARK III ARRANGEMENT OF CHASSIS FOR COACHBUILDER. MODEL 9613E. 16'-4" WHEELBASE. 8'-0" OVERALL WIDTH.

9·6 LITRE ENGINE
FLUID TRANSMISSION
AIR PRESSURE BRAKES.

DRAWING No. 12

This drawing of the 9613E chassis was issued on 29th December 1949, five months before the increase in maximum length to 27ft. came into effect. In practice, it was not until the autumn of 1950 that examples began to enter service. The chassis design was identical to that of the 9612E apart from the extra overhang — the drawing is reproduced to 4mm scale.

Chapter five:
Enter the 27ft. Regent models 1950-57

John Rackham retired in June 1950 and one wonders whether he might have pressed for the Regent IV project to be further developed had this not been so. However, it was perhaps fitting that the last production double-decker with which he was associated was the highly successful Regent III, of which the final series had been approved for production the previous winter, when it became known that the maximum length for two-axle double-deckers was to be increased from the previous 26ft. to 27ft., with effect from 1st June 1950. General operation of 8ft.-wide buses was also approved from that date.

The increase in length was dealt with very simply, by adding to the rear overhang, no alteration being made to the wheelbase length of 16ft. 4in., nor in other respects to the chassis as a whole. The 9.6-litre model designations changed from 9612E and 9612A to 9613E and 9613A while the 7.7-litre version went from 6811A to 6812A. The 26ft. models continued to be listed as current within the drawing office, more for administrative convenience than any expectation of

The traditional Leeds City Transport representation at the Commercial Motor Show was maintained by No. 700, one of the earliest examples of the 9613E series of Regent III, complete with 8ft.-wide Roe bodywork in the four-bay tradition begun in 1937. However, it was displayed with Crossley nameplates, the ACV group having just begun its badge engineering era so far as Earls Court vehicles were concerned. This photograph was taken in October 1950 outside the AEC works just after the vehicle had been fitted with its permanent AEC nameplates on return from the Show and shortly before delivery to Leeds. The chassis, 9613E2455, bore the last in the sequence of 120 numbers booked when Leeds reserved this quantity of vehicles for delivery commencing in 1948 and which included the 8ft.-wide Show vehicle that year, 9612E2355. The 1952 Show exhibit, again generally similar but 7ft. 6in. wide, took the fleet number 800 originally applied to the Regent IV shown opposite.

continued demand, except of course for the RT which continued completely undisturbed in 26ft. form as type O961. The overseas 17ft. 6in. wheelbase model also continued unchanged, retaining the 9612E designation.

However, though the change of model number had only the dimensional significance mentioned above, there were other developments around the same time which altered the specification appreciably. It was apparent that the A208 engine could overheat when driven fairly hard, it being discovered that not enough of the cooled water from the radiator was reaching the rearmost cylinders. This was solved by adding an external water pipe feeding coolant to the back of the cylinder head and standard right-hand 9.6-litre engines built with this were designated A218, becoming standard from about 1949. The A204 engine used on the O961 RT model did not change type number although it too was altered - London Transport decided to carry out the conversion on existing engines and therefore did not need to make the distinction. The 9.6-litre engine was proving very reliable and with this work done its performance could be used fully when needed without running into problems.

A more obvious if less important change was the adoption of a cast aluminium radiator in place of the previous chromium-plated pressed-shell type which had proved vulnerable to minor damage, scratching, etc. This reversion to earlier practice roughly coincided with the introduction of the 9613-series models, though not directly related to that change - here again, the O961 was not affected, always having had an aluminium radiator casing.

It is not easy to be specific about quoting a chassis number changeover point for the 27ft. models, though the City of Oxford batch with PWL registration numbers beginning at 9613A5615 is perhaps as near as one can get. The problem is not only the usual AEC one of chassis production not necessarily being strictly in sequence of number allocation, but compounded by the big allocations to London Transport. At about this period, AEC's department responsible for allocating chassis numbers on confirmation of orders began to work on a basis of filling in gaps that had arisen due to cancelled orders. As a result various 9613-series chassis received numbers which were wildly out of place by normal standards. They were slotted into appropriate sized gaps as opportunity arose from about 1951 right up to 1955. Space does not permit giving full details but the lowest such number was 9613A1330, built for the National Coal Board in 1953, while 9613A1646-9 were built for Welsh municipalities in 1951-52, 9613A2586-99 for Devon General in 1951 and the 2680-99 block went to Sheffield, Huddersfield, Bury and GNR (Eire) in 1952, some being 9613A and others 9613E. Leeds City Transport's 1950 batch 9613E2432-55 (the last-mentioned a 1950 Show exhibit temporarily bearing Crossley plates) and South Wales 9613A4595-4617 of 1951, hardly count, being pre-arranged delayed deliveries following on numerically from earlier batches for the same fleets.

Nottingham City Transport placed an order for some 112 9612E buses with Park Royal bodywork that were originally due to begin delivery around the beginning of 1950 and would have

been 9612E4831-4942, but were held back mainly by constructional problems with a new garage. It was agreed that 72 would be built in 1953-54 and these emerged as 9613E4831-4902 even though the bodywork was built to the original design and was thus 26ft. long. A further ten were built in 1954 as 9613S4903-12, with the synchromesh gearbox described later in this chapter, but the rest were cancelled in favour of Regent V models, as described in Chapter Seven. Some of the resulting blank numbers were used up as 9613E4913-20 and 9613E4923-32 for Huddersfield in 1954-55 and 9613S4921 went to Bevan & Barker in 1954 but others were never used — there were also a handful of other blanks in the 961 series.

Operators were becoming increasingly conscious of running costs in the face of growing pressure for higher wages and the revival of private motoring with the ending of petrol rationing. The latter was yet to have much impact but fuel economy was again becoming of importance in the choice of buses. A Gardner 6LW engine was the subject of extended tests to probe the secrets of its good results during this period, though it was yet to be considered as a production option. The 9.6-litre engine was generally preferred - sales of 6812A models still being sluggish, barely getting into double figures in the 1950-53 period - but the conventional clutch and gearbox had regained wider favour. Not only was the 9613A the universal choice among BET companies but it was also favoured by some prominent municipalities which had chosen epicyclic models at least for a time, such as Liverpool and Sheffield.

There may well have been

The use of 'old' numbers for new chassis gave rise to some confusion in the early 'fifties. Chassis numbers around 1600 in the 961 series had originally been allocated in the 1947-48 period but cancelled orders had left some blanks which were among those filled at a time when most new chassis had numbers over 7000. This example had chassis number 9613A1649 but was built early in 1952 for Bedwas & Machen Urban District Council. Not all operators favoured the 8ft. width by then general and this vehicle was 7ft. 6in. wide, as were three similar buses supplied a few months earlier to nearby Aberdare UDC and allocated the immediately preceding numbers 9613A1646-8, all having Northern Counties bodywork. The cast aluminium radiator shown was by then standard. The nearside headlamp was evidently still awaited when this picture was taken in June 1952.

(Below)Fire engines were built on what amounted to shortened 9613A chassis in 1951-53 for Merryweather, but they were produced under Maudslay auspices and most did not have AEC-type chassis numbers. Park Royal built the bodywork, the example shown being for Nottinghamshire.

(Centre right) The 27ft. 6812A 7.7-litre version of the Regent III sold in very small numbers in 1951-53, with only three customers — the municipalities of Morecambe, Lowestoft and Colchester. One of Lowestoft's pair of vehicles dating from 1951, No. 28 (LBJ 743) on chassis 6812A106 is seen here. The 58-seat bodywork was built by Massey Bros of Wigan.

One source of 'spare' chassis numbers was a Nottingham City Transport order for 112 vehicles originally intended to begin delivery in 1950 but reduced to 72 and held back to 1953-54. The Park Royal bodywork was built to the original planned design and thus nominally obsolete by the time the vehicles were built, though, like most double-deckers of the period, being well-proportioned and neatly finished. The chassis were 9613E-type but the completed buses conformed to the old 26ft. length limit, though 8ft. wide, standard in Nottingham from 1949. Number 159, seen here, was on chassis 9613E4863 and entered service in February 1954.

Noteworthy among those who switched from preselective transmission was Sheffield, where Corporation and Joint Committee fleets had favoured the 9612E but switched to the Leyland PD2 synchromesh model until AEC advised that it was introducing a synchromesh version of the Regent. The first nine vehicles supplied were delivered in September-October 1952 with crash gearboxes, the new unit not being ready in time. They had Roe bodywork, at that stage also still unfamiliar in the Sheffield fleet, though one batch of Leyland PD2/12 with similar bodies had entered service the previous year, the livery in both cases being a slightly non-standard version of Sheffield's striking cream and blue. Number 118, on chassis 9613A2687, is seen posed for its bodybuilder's official picture immediately in front of the drawing office where many fine-looking and durable vehicles were designed. The letter B below the fleet number signified that this bus was in the Corporation and British Railways-owned part of the Joint Committee fleet. Number 119 of the same batch was exhibited on the Roe stand at the Earls Court Show that year.

subsequent regret at this decision in some cases as the venerable D124 'crash' gearbox was beginning to show its limitations. When it was introduced in 1931, the gross weight for a two-axle double-decker had just been increased to 10 tons but a typical 1951 Regent III with 27ft. by 8ft. body was often running close to the 12-ton limit then in force with unladen weight around 8 tons. Moreover the 9.6-litre engine's increased torque could impose severe loadings, especially if clumsily used and breakages began to be reported too frequently for comfort. AEC was developing a new synchromesh gearbox but a stop-gap measure was the introduction of the D162, very like the D124 and still with the sliding-mesh engagement of first and second gear that was at the heart of the problem but with these pairs of gears

widened. It became standard for the 9613A in June 1951, but the alteration made little difference, tooth breakages and even splitting of second gear continuing.

When it was borne in mind that the fuel saving over the 9613E was rarely if ever more than 1 mpg in directly comparable situations, even a few such failures with their attendant costs could soon swallow up the apparent savings. What's more, the preselctive transmission had been improved and was even more reliable by this date. Yet AEC had been casting envious eyes on the market attractions of Leyland's synchromesh transmission on the PD2 model, even though it was known at Southall that there had been problems with that, too. It was ironical that Leyland was meanwhile becoming convinced that epicyclic gearboxes held

the key to the future - a classic case of the other man's grass always seeming to be greener.

It was Leyland, incidentally, who in querying the balancing of fluid flywheels being supplied for the special versions of the PD2 built to RT specification for London Transport, caused standards to be improved on AEC's own vehicles, eliminating a 'shivering' type of vibration which had afflicted a proportion of earlier preselective Regent III models.

There was much interest both in transmission development and fuel economy generally at this time. The experimental department at Southall used one Regent chassis, 9612A2611, almost continuously for gearbox work. In its early days it had a Brockhouse turbo-transmitter as offered on Crossley models, possibly as a

The traditional combination of Weymann-bodied Regents in maroon livery continued to be favoured by Devon General, Rhondda and South Wales, three BET companies whose vehicle policy had long had much in common. Rhondda's 1952 batch of fourteen had 9613A chassis with the 'wide-tooth' D162 gearbox and the outswept skirt panels associated with this body style were confined to the space between the axles. Number 261 (LNY 342) was on chassis 9613A7061 and is seen soon after entering service in April of that year. The lack of cream relief to what was really a somewhat sombre choice of colour seemed acceptable on this elegant design.

consequence of the take-over of Crossley Motors, but soon after I joined AEC as a draughtsman in the latter part of 1951 it was being used for testing a prototype synchromesh unit - I have a note that it was in use so fitted on 10th March 1952, reverting to a D124 crash unit by 4th April, probably for comparative tests. It was also used for other purposes and remained in the experimental fleet until the late 'fifties, being ultimately sold to Cream Line of Bordon and fitted with a Roe forward-entrance lowbridge body for use by its Liss & District subsidiary.

This chassis may have been another, fairly early, instance of gap-filling in the chassis number series, and ten vehicles placed in service by Trent Motor Traction in June 1950 were possibly others. They were fitted with Crossley synchromesh gearboxes and were given chassis numbers 9612X2600-09. This was no more than a passing phase and in August 1952 the AEC synchromesh gearbox for Regent III chassis, type D166, was added to the list of options available. It was derived from the D159 unit recently introduced for the Regal IV underfloor-engined single-decker but in this case was arranged to bolt directly behind the engine.

The chassis model was designated 9613S, but the two chassis which were to appear as bodied exhibits at the Commercial Motor Show which were to be the first new vehicles with this unit had already been built and were thus 9613A as displayed. Both, as it happened, also had new bonnet designs and thus figure prominently in that aspect of the Regent story, as will be described in the next chapter.

AEC had been experimenting with its own synchromesh gearboxes since the late 'thirties, but chose not to make such units generally available until 1952-53. This 1937 Regent, originally one of five with preselective transmission and Metro-Cammell bodywork placed in service by Birmingham City Transport, was one of a number of vehicles of that period converted with experimental synchromesh units (Liverpool, Nottingham and London Transport being other users). It had been sold in 1951 and is seen here when owned by Harvey of Cottenham, Cambridgeshire, outside AEC's experimental department when borrowed back for reassessment in March 1952, AEC trade plates being attached.

Crossley had already introduced a synchromesh gearbox for its bus range when taken over by AEC and so when Trent Motor Traction Co Ltd wanted this form of gearbox for its 1950 fleet additions, 20 Regal 7.7-litre and ten Regent 9.6-litre chassis were built with examples of this unit, the gearbox symbol in the chassis designation being X. The Regent models were 8ft. wide, the frontal appearance of the Willowbrook 56-seat bodywork looking much more massive than the earlier 7ft. 6in. version used on Regent II — it was also of four-bay construction, with deep lower-deck windows. Number 1203 (BRC 403) on chassis 9612X2603 is seen leaving Nottingham when newly in service in June 1950. Despite the gearbox exercise, AEC subsequently lost Trent as a regular customer — Leyland obtained all orders from this company for new vehicles for the remainder of the 'fifties.

BET companies were among the first to receive production Regent III models with the synchromesh gearbox. City of Oxford Motor Services Ltd took delivery of fifteen 9613S in 1953, divided equally between normal-height Park Royal and lowbridge Weymann batches - when originally placed, this order had been for 9613A types. Number 927 (TWL 927) on chassis 9613S7213, one of the Park Royal examples, is seen passing All Souls College. Oxford buses of this era, with their well-proportioned appearance and distinctive livery, suited the city's dignified architecture.

Nottingham City Transport, faced with a requirement for lowbridge buses to operate a new service, took a further ten vehicles from its long-delayed 1950 order, delivered in April-June 1954. The chassis specified was altered to the synchromesh-gearbox 9613S and Park Royal built the bodywork to its contemporary standards. Number 201 (SAU 201) is on chassis 9613S4905. Nottingham had long been a stronghold of preselective transmission but was among quite a number of municipalities which decided that the prospect of fuel economy justified a switch to 'manual' gearboxes, despite the increased effort required from the driver.

One of the two, 9613A7173, for Devon General, received the hand-built prototype gearbox produced by the craftsmen in AEC's experimental department. It was delivered and ran faultlessly on some of the operator's hilly routes, encouraging prospects for production. Unfortunately, this was not maintained and many early D166 synchromesh gearboxes were soon the subject of complaint, just as had been the case with earlier Leyland and Crossley ventures in this direction. The AEC unit's problems - mainly a tendency to jump out of gear - proved to be related to production manufacturing methods and were corrected fairly quickly. The AEC gearbox design differed from Leyland's in providing synchromesh for all four forward gears, a feature then found on very few car gearboxes, and indeed Leyland was on the point of retreating

in the sense of providing this feature only on third and top gears. On the other hand the AEC unit had straight-toothed gears throughout and gave little or no improvement on the previous 'crash' units in terms of quietness, which was very much inferior to Leyland's helical-geared design.

Even so, once the seemingly inevitable teething troubles (unintenional pun!) were overcome, the AEC D166 synchromesh gearbox was effective and favoured by many operators for over a decade, being retained for 9.6-litre-engined Mark V models.

However, what might be called the hard core of epicyclic gearbox users remained loyal. Leeds comes immediately to mind and it is amusing to recall that adoption of a larger-diameter exhaust system in the

interests of fuel economy prompted protests from the local watch committee around 1952. The standard 9613E, like previous provincial preselector models, was if anything quieter than the London RT, the standard 2½in. diameter exhaust note of both being decidedly 'soft' and the provincial models perhaps emitting marginally less direct engine noise due to the different air cleaner and bonnet design. The 3in. exhaust gave what can best be described as a 'motor boat' note, certainly far less obtrusive than was to be heard in nearby and rather 'posh' Harrogate, where the West Yorkshire Road Car Co Ltd was one of several Tilling companies applying similar ideas to Bristol K5G models on local town services, considerably noisier in the first place and positively raucous as modified. There were other, mainly municipal, users of the 9613E

and several of the other Yorkshire municipalities - Bradford, Halifax, Huddersfield and Hull - were prominent.

By far the biggest user of the preselective Regent III remained London Transport, of course, which continued to place big orders for O961-model chassis for its RT fleet. The 'thousand-off' batch of 1949-50 was never repeated, but a total of 2,304 RT chassis were built with chassis numbers in seven blocks of various lengths between O9615045 and O9618084 over the period between July 1950 and September 1954, among smaller numbers of provincial models. The largest single consecutive run over that period was O9615721-6387, amounting to 667 chassis, presumably 'two-thirds of a thousand', but the other batches varied between round-figure numbers and less obvious totals, the smallest being the final 112. In practice, RT chassis production was a continuous process, with about eight to ten going down the production line every week, popular with the workers because they were so well developed that assembly was invariably trouble-free, and good bonus money a certainty. A London Transport inspector - who incidentally drove to work daily in his black Ford Popular car of about 1935 (the £100 model)

Other urban operators remained firm in their view that fluid transmission was the better proposition. Among them was Ipswich Corporation, which had begun conversion of its hitherto all-trolleybus route network to motor buses in 1950, choosing the preselective Regent III, doubtless partly influenced by the greater ease of retraining former trolleybus drivers. Number 13 (CDX 513), on chassis 9613E7960, was one of the second batch of four Regents delivered in April 1954, complete with Park Royal 56-seat bodywork. Although the Regent III was nominally to become obsolete later that year with the introduction of the Regent V, Ipswich was to take two further batches, receiving the last four examples of the 9.6-litre version to be built in July 1956. All were 7ft. 6in.-wide.

Another user of 7ft. 6in.-wide 9613E models was London Transport, for the second batch of 56 RLH-type lowbridge double-deckers introduced in 1952 were based on chassis nominally of this type, even though the Weymann bodywork was of 26ft. overall length and virtually identical to the 20 earlier vehicles based on 9612E chassis placed in service in 1950. The vehicle shown, RLH 53 (MXX 253) on chassis 9613E6976, was the first of the final two dozen which were in red livery for use on two central area routes requiring low-height buses, the remainder being green for country services. This view shows the seating layout particularly well — forward vision from the upper deck was not a strong point. Though the chassis was still of 'provincial' type in all major respects, the 1952 batch incorporated rather more of LTE practice in minor features.

Production of RT-type buses for London Transport slowed down somewhat in 1951, though a further impressive batch of some 667 consecutively-numbered chassis were going through the works at Southall throughout the year. One of them, O9615773 is seen here in Sidcup after bodying by Weymann as country area RT4046 and entering service in February 1951. The fleet numbers issued to Weymann-bodied RT buses tended to be well ahead of those appearing at the same time from Park Royal because of the latter's involvement in bodying RTL-type Leyland chassis, and the registration numbers were a better guide to age, broadly speaking.

The sight of a shiny new RT, often lacking some of its advertisements for the first few weeks, was still impressive. Here RT3002, on chassis O9616893, is seen soon after delivery from Park Royal in May 1953, at Muswell Hill on route 244 which had previously been operated by single-deckers. Despite its modest fleet number, this was one of the last few hundred bodies to appear from Park Royal, having bodywork of type RT8/2, the final version of the 'standard' RT, as built by both Park Royal and Weymann, outwardly very similar to the RT3/1 and the RT8 which had been built in huge numbers since 1948, when the roof-mounted route number box was dropped. There were minor internal structural differences in the three types, but together they could be found on three-quarters of the post-war RT buses.

Ironically, the last registration number series allocated to RT-type buses was OLD, and as well as appearing on the last vehicles of what was by then an old-established type there was a further sense in which it was apt for 110 of the 160 new RT chassis which received 'old' bodies transferred from the unsuccessful SRT-class (conversions from pre-war STL-type Regent O661-type chasis into RT look-alikes). The vehicle shown, RT4500, received the 1949 Park Royal body from SRT99. entering service in April 1954, and was one of those with bodies repainted in Green Line livery for use on the routes running eastward from Aldgate. The chassis, O9617960, was one of the final batch of RT chassis produced by AEC.

kept in 'as new' condition -was permanently stationed at the AEC works to check them over, but his job was very much a routine one. It came as quite a shock when it all came to an end on 16th September 1954 with the delivery of the final chassis, O9618084, which as it happened became RT4554, a Weymann-bodied green country area vehicle completed almost immediately but stored until May 1955 - the highest numbered vehicle of this type, RT4825, had entered service in March 1954, having been bodied by Park Royal.

Some 4,674 post-war RT buses had been delivered to London Transport, all with virtually identical 3RT-type chassis. This was an unrivalled intake of buses to one chassis design, and

except for those with Cravens bodywork, almost uniform in body design. As it turned out, there were really too many, especially if the 2,131 Leyland chassis to RT specification were added - even though orders had latterly been cut back, falling demand for services meant that London Transport did not need all these excellent new buses. Within a few years some were being sold off, yet over half the AEC chassis were to remain in London service at the end of 1970, over sixteen years after the last one had been built and even then many of these were over 20 years old. Some of the last to survive were nominally over 30 years old and even though London Transport's overhaul methods in effect

mixed their components, a genuine operational life of over quarter of a century was to be quite commonplace towards the end.

Meanwhile, the final years of the Regent III era were taking a different turn. Interest in lighter buses had grown since the appearance of the Daimler CLG5 double-decker and Leyland Tiger Cub single-decker at the 1952 Show. AEC was about to introduce its own medium weight range including the single-deck Reliance model, of which the prototype had just been built, but, as an interim measure, partly to help in assessing demand, a prototype lightweight double-decker using Mark III components was built. It was

Interest in weight reduction increased considerably in 1952-53 and AEC built a 7.7-litre prototype, basically similar to the 6812A but to lightweight specification and with synchromesh gearbox. Park Royal contributed most to the weight saving, yet retained external appearance almost unchanged from the standard product and neat if plain internal finish. Registered 7194 H, painted in Oxford livery and delivered in August 1953, it visited quite a number of operators, being seen when working for Nottingham City Transport in January 1954, in company with a 1937 Cravens-bodied Regent still in service with that undertaking and representing an early application of the same engine type.

Rhondda Transport Ltd, like most BET-group operators, soon began to adopt lightweight construction. A batch of six Regent III delivered in January 1954 carried Weymann bodywork to the austere Orion design then newly in production, including No. 284 (NTG 137) on chassis 9613S7760 and seen here — the days of classical elegance were over for this fleet. A year later further Weymann bodies of generally similar design but with seating capacity increased from 56 to 60 were mounted on ten 6813S-type chassis, the only examples of this model built, apart from the demonstrator shown at the top.

The appearance of the 6813S seemed to have a modest stimulant effect on demand for the existing 7.7-litre 6812A model. In 1954, examples were placed in service by three operators, including West Bridgford UDC, hitherto a user of the 9.6-litre preselective-gearbox version of the Regent III. Two vehicles with lowbridge 55-seat bodywork were ordered for the same Clifton service for which Nottingham had ordered the 9613S models illustrated in page 46. The body contract went to Willowbrook, again a departure, for WBUDC had been a consistent Park Royal customer. The chassis number, 6812A086-7, were another instance of gap-filling, neighbouring numbers dating from 1948-49 — West Bridgford 11 (ORR 139), the first of the pair, is seen in 1957 with a Nottingham Daimler CVD6. The WBUDC fleet was taken over by Nottingham in 1968. Happily the other vehicle of the pair is now restored to original livery.

For the last batches of its bodywork on Regent III chassis, Park Royal reverted to slightly deeper windows in both decks, reducing the resemblance to the RT design somewhat. This was in fact basically the body design as introduced for the Regent V at 1954 Earls Court Show, and even on this chassis the total unladen weight came out as a modest 7 tons 5 cwt, despite the shapely and 'solid' appearance. The vehicle seen here was one of the last Regent III models to be supplied to an independent operator, being delivered to J. W. Camplin of Donington, near Spalding, Lincolnshire, in May 1955. Most of the

Mark III series buses supplied in 1955-56 had 'new-look' front-end, of one type or another, but this vehicle was among the minority with the traditional style, generally resembling the final Ipswich batches though in this case on synchromesh chassis 9613S8170. Camplin's fleet, operated under the Holme Delight fleetname, in those days consisted of seven vehicles with only a pair of double-deckers, both Park Royal-bodied Regent III, used on its Spalding to Boston service.

derived from the 6812A and had the 7.7-litre A173 engine, D166 synchromesh gearbox and various lightweight chassis components, though most of these, such as smaller-size tyres and a smaller fuel tank, were related to the planned lighter body weight.

The model designation for this special Regent III was 6813S, though the prototype chassis was numbered U163996. Park Royal built a neatly-finished 58-seat body to its usual contemporary outline but based on a new lightweight aluminium-alloy structure, the complete vehicle delivered back to AEC in August 1953 weighing 6 tons 12 cwt 1 qr, 1½ tons less than some similar-looking buses on 9613A chassis for Oxford, whose livery it shared. It was registered in Middlesex, as usual with AEC demonstrators, receiving the number 7194H at a time when 'reversed' numbers were still unfamiliar in most parts of the country it was about to tour. It created a favourable impression, with little of the austerity of some lightweight vehicles of that

era, its weight-saving features being more evenly balanced.

It was never intended to build 6813S models in any quantity, manufacture of the 7.7-litre engine being about to cease, and 7194H served its purpose well in confirming the existence of a market for such a vehicle, before being sold in October 1954 to Mayne of Droylsden, Manchester, a Regent user since 1934. In the event, Rhondda Transport, a regular Regent customer since 1933, did take delivery of ten similar chassis, 6813S117-126, at the beginning of 1955, though these had Weymann Orion bodywork. By that date, the first Regent V medium weight models had been built, but with hindsight, Rhondda probably got a more reliable proposition.

Construction of both 9.6-litre and standard 7.7-litre models continued and it was not until 1956 that the last of the former entered service. Appropriately, it was a 'proper' Regent III with preselective transmission and air brakes that was numerically the last in the 961 series, 9613E8261 being the last of a batch of four for Ipswich

Corporation, which like several of the smaller municipalities had stuck to the 7ft. 6in. width. It was No. 24 in that fleet (EPV 24). They entered service in July 1956, the same month as some of Sheffield's last 9613S models with immediately preceding numbers - Sheffield was the largest of the operators placing Regent III buses in service as late as 1955-56, though they looked like Mark V models, as explained in the next chapter.

As it turned out, Reading Corporation was, strictly speaking, the final Regent III customer, the last four of nine 6812A models being placed in service in January 1957, the final vehicle being 6821A136. Somehow one did not entirely accept this 7.7-litre version of the model as a 'real' Mark III, even though it had its own tradition, Reading having been a customer for 7.7-litre Regents since 1935, and the gearbox emitting the unmistakable sound that had been familiar for even longer.

Not only the inspiration but the practical execution of the decision to adopt Birmingham City Transport's 'New Look' style for 40 Regent III buses for Bradford Corporation owed much to Crossley's involvement in the development of that design. The Crossley-manufactured front cowl and bonnet were virtually as used on the Birmingham version and the front mudguards of similar design but adapted to 8ft.-width. It is noteworthy that

Mr Chaceley Humpidge, then the Bradford undertaking's General Manager, evidently favoured the Birmingham package in other details, such as the use of the municipal coat of arms as a radiator badge, displacing the AEC triangle to the bottom, and the recessed windscreen, giving a rather severe line to the East Lancashire bodywork. Number 75, on chassis 9613E7113, was one of the first dozen, seen soon after entering service in November 1952.

Chapter six:
New look Regents, 1952-56

In February 1950, Birmingham City Transport caused quite a stir with the appearance of its 'New Look' front-end design with concealed radiator and bonnet wider than usual hitherto, to be applied to Daimler, Guy and Crossley buses then on order. The first example was a Crossley, the initial vehicle of the final 100 of an order for 260 buses on SD42/6 chassis for which Crossley also supplied the bodywork. Daimler and Guy subsequently adopted the design as standard and quite a wide variety of operators decided to favour this or similar styles.

When Bradford Corporation placed an order for 40 AEC Regent III chassis numbered 9613E7089-7128 which were to have a front-end of this style, for delivery beginning in the latter part of 1952, it was decided to follow the practice that had been adopted for the Midland Red Regent II models built in 1946-47 as described in Chapter One to

the extent that the chassis were fitted with 'plain' radiators without decorative shells and the bonnet and mudguards omitted. The chassis were

then sent to Crossley at Stockport, where they received what were virtually Birmingham-style front-end sheet metalwork before proceeding to

The first bus to be completed to the design so widely copied had been Birmingham's No. 2426, placed in service in February 1950, one of an order for 260 Crossley SD42/6 models with Crossley bodywork for that fleet, though only the last hundred were of the New Look type, so christened in line with new developments in women's fashions. They were the only Crossley buses of this style, soon to become more associated with Daimler and Guy buses both for Birmingham and elsewhere.

Concealed radiator styling was very much the 'in' thing at the 1952 Commercial Motor Show, most of the double-deckers on display having this feature in one form or another. Among AEC exhibits, pride of place was taken by this Regent III, Devon General DR679 (NTT 679), the last of a batch of 20 9613A models with Weymann bodywork, but differing from the remainder in both the Birmingham-style front-end of the chassis and the special body design, given the name Aurora. This body, retaining the traditional Weymann curved profile but having a new combination of deep lower-deck and shallow upper-deck windows, the former with curved outline at front and rear ends, was to remain unique as the harsher Orion concept took over. This was the vehicle used for trials with the pre-production prototype D166 synchromesh gearbox though it had started life with a crash gearbox, being numbered 9613A7173 but later becoming 9613S7173 accordingly. It is seen in service at Plymouth.

Blackburn where the East Lancashire bodywork was built. The first dozen entered service on 1st November.

However, in the meanwhile, the last vehicle from a slightly later order for 20 9612A models for the Devon General fleet was earmarked as an exhibit for the Commercial Motor Show held in September-October 1952 and this, too, was to have the Crossley-made new-look front end as well as a new style of Weymann body, this being 9613A7173, the bus afterwards used to test the prototype D166 synchromesh gearbox as mentioned in the last chapter. It was thus displayed before the Bradford vehicles had entered

service and could hence be described as the first Regent to appear publicly with this style of front end.

At the same Show, however, the first example of a different version of wide-bonnet concealed radiator styling appeared on the Crossley stand. This was the first of a batch of 100 chassis for Liverpool, numbered 9613A7610 (the wide gap from the directly contemporary Devon General vehicle's number being mainly due to a 375-vehicle London order). In this case, the bodywork was also by Crossley and a full-width bonnet was employed in place of the Birmingham 'three-quarter width' style, though the grille

was similar. The vehicle carried Crossley chassis nameplates as displayed but these were removed and standard AEC plates fitted before delivery, the opportunity also being taken to fit a synchromesh gearbox, installed from new on the remainder of the batch. Two of these 100 went to Saunders-Roe for bodying but the remainder had Crossley bodies or Crossley shells for completion by Liverpool.

However, the Birmingham-pattern front reappeared for a batch of six 9613E for Hull and a repeat order for twelve 9613S for Devon General completed in October 1953 and June

Over on Crossley's stand at the same 1952 Show was the vehicle shown here, Liverpool Corporation's A1 (NKD 501). It was officially called a Crossley Regent for that event as part of the ACV group's somewhat childish pretence aimed at increasing its representation at Shows during the 1950-56 period, but at least it was genuinely in part a Crossley product. As well as the body, Crossley was responsible on this as on the other early New Look Regents, for the visible parts of the chassis sheet metalwork. In this case, the bonnet and front cowl width were extended to suit the full 8ft. width of the body, though the grille was of the same shape as on the Birmingham-style version. The vehicle was the first of 100 with similar front-end design, which remained unique to Liverpool. This bus did not enter service until June 1953, by which date it had not only received its correct AEC nameplates, but had also received a synchromesh gearbox, the chassis number becoming 9613S7610.

Kingston upon Hull Corporation was perhaps a likely candidate for the concealed-radiator style in view of its continued use of the 'streamlined' livery introduced in the 'thirties. This photograph of No. 338 (OKH 338) on chassis 9613E7749 shows how AEC's version of this front-end was intended to carry the triangular badge in its traditional place, though it is noteworthy that the space at the bottom of the grille used on the Bradford version remained blank instead of being eliminated as on the Liverpool version. These six vehicles, placed in service in October 1953, had the traditional Weymann style of bodywork, which matched the curves of the front-end of the chassis better than more straight-framed styles. Little concession to lighter construction was made with an unladen weight of 7 tons 19 cwt 1 qr.

1954 respectively. By that time work was in hand for the front-end for the new Regent V range described in the next chapter and as there was an overlap of production of the Mark III and Mark V models the inevitable happened - combination of the Regent V front-end on the Regent III (9613S to be precise) chassis. The customer was Sheffield, for whose Corporation and Joint Committee fleets some 86 such vehicles were built, entering service between July 1955 and July 1956.

Devon General followed up its 1952 Show vehicle with an order for twelve similar chassis, complete with the London pattern of rear wheel discs also favoured on the Bradford buses. The Weymann bodywork, however, was of the five-bay Orion lightweight design which seemed decidedly austere by comparison with that on earlier Regent III models in this fleet. They were delivered in June 1954 and DR 733 (PDV 733) on chassis 9613S8099 is seen just over a year later in Sidmouth.

The Regent III 'faded away' rather than dying abruptly after the introduction of its Mark V successor — the 9613E and 9613S were still included in the data sheet for 1955 issued in August 1954. In fact, of the final 90 chassis in the 961 model series, placed in service between July 1955 and a year later, all but the last four even looked like the standard Regent V models by then in full production. Sheffield specified the Mark V-style front-end for these 86 9613S models for its municipal and joint committee fleets, with bodywork by Roe or Weymann. Seen here is chassis number 9613S8257 No. 1291 (WWB 491), numerically the last 9.6-litre Regent III apart from Ipswich's final four. The Weymann body seated 55, the vehicle being one of a batch of nine purchased to convert three Sheffield Joint Omnibus Committee routes previously run by single-deckers, the owner of this particular 'railway' vehicle being quoted on the side as British Transport Commission. It is noteworthy that 45 of these buses supplied to Sheffield Corporation's own undertaking replaced an order for 45 Leyland PD2/20, cancelled when Leyland advised that it was no longer offering synchromesh on second gear.

Chapter seven:
The Regent V takes over 1954-56

Much of the early publicity on the Regent Mark V range was, understandably, centered on the lightweight successor to the 6813S that had acted as a market survey experiment - two examples of this new model were built and bodied for the 1954 Commercial Motor Show. Yet from the start it was a complete range designed to take over from the Mark III series. The official announcement was made on the 14th September 1954, a couple of days before the last RT chassis left the Southall factory.

These two events were related in a more complex way than merely the new taking over from the old. London Transport already had more new buses than it needed, yet work on a successor to the RT, of advanced design, had reached the stage of the first prototype also being completed for the 1954 Show, this being the prototype Routemaster, RM1. It was based on experimental work, some involving RT-type buses, going back about six years. Inevitably, it took the limelight, with lengthy descriptions in the technical press of its integral construction, independent front suspension, power-hydraulic brake system, power-assisted steering, and numerous other features. It occupied pride of place on AEC's stand, yet it was clear that bulk orders would not be forthcoming for some time.

Had this not been so, there might have been more chance of keeping London and provincial bus design at AEC more closely related, as had hitherto been achieved quite effectively, despite what could almost be described as cosmetic differences. The Routemaster and the Regent V range had almost nothing in common apart from an original engine and transmission option on the latter, and even this was only true in general terms, with many detail differences.

By that date, operators outside London were looking for economy and in many cases prepared to accept a more austere type of bus to achieve it yet London Transport's engineers were also seeking cost savings but on a more long-term time scale. Reconciling the two might have been possible, and one wonders whether John Rackham, always in favour of standardisation of as many parts as possible, might have achieved it had he still been AEC's Chief Engineer.

As it was, there were several conflicting strands of influence on design. Within AEC, A. J. Romer had been appointed Managing Director in August 1950. Previously, he had been General Manager of the Bristol bus chassis plant and, as an engineer, was involved in AEC design policy to a greater extent than had been the case with AEC's top management in the Rackham era - George Robinson, promoted to be Rackham's successor, was still 'No. 2' to some extent. A younger generation was represented by

R. A. (Bob) Fryars, Assistant Chief Engineer, who had been largely responsible for the mediumweight Mercury goods and Reliance underfloor-engined single-deck models introduced the previous year.

The BET group of operating companies favoured the lightweight approach, having already placed several orders for Reliance models, some for fleets not previously associated with AEC. The term 'mediumweight' was favoured at AEC, the letter M being used as a prefix in the new model designation based mainly on letters, so the new light Regent V was type MD3RV, signifying 'mediumweight, double-decker, synchromesh, right-hand, vacuum brakes'. Ironically, the one feature previously denoted by letter was now indicated by a figure, 3 being used for synchromesh and 2 for epicyclic models.

The MD3RV was, in effect, a modernised version of the 6813S, using the new AV470 engine from the Mercury range and a lighter synchromesh gearbox also derived from that range, but with four speeds instead of five. The AV470 had a swept volume of 7.685 litres, fractionally more than the true 7.58 litres of the previous '7.7' and was in many ways different in design, beyond being an in-line six-cylinder unit with the same toroidal direct-injection system. In particular, it revived the wet cylinder

It was over a year later that the first production MD3RV models entered service. The South Wales Transport Co Ltd took delivery of 20 with chassis numbers immediately after the two 1954 Show examples, all bodied by Weymann to the standard MCW Orion design, by then well established. Ten were of lowbridge layout, with what had previously generally been the traditional highbridge seating capacity of 56, with 30 upstairs and 26 down, and MD3RV021 (South Wales No. 458) is seen here posed for AEC's official picture in October 1955 — it entered service with most of the rest of the batch the following month. Note the external radiator filler, with curiously long neck, which had meanwhile been adopted. The markedly offset front wheels were usually a clue to the MD-series chassis in 8ft.-wide form. The Orion body was much more obviously lightweight than Park Royal's version, yet the weight, 6.10.2, was almost identical.

liner principle used in a none-too-successful pre-war engine fitted in the Regal Mark II single-decker of 1936-39 (see No. 6 in this series). The cylinder dimensions were 112 mm by 130mm, which made it more naturally a faster-revving engine than the long-stroke A173, but the economy rating of 103 bhp at 1800 rpm recommended for this application was only marginally more powerful - maximum power available was 112 bhp at 2000 rpm.

The new standard front-end styling had obvious resemblances to the previous 'Birmingham new-look' pattern, but had a new radiator grille, following traditional AEC practice in having the triangular radiator badge set in a polished surround but broader and shallower in line with contemporary car trends and lacking the subtle curves of the familiar radiator outline, particularly in the area around the badge. The over-centre bonnet closing mechanism of the Mark III version was retained. Alternatively, the entire Mark III type of radiator, bonnet and front wings were offered as an option, reflecting the preference of many customers. All models were also available in 7ft. 6in.-wide form, though 8ft. width was standard by this date.

Less attention tended to be focussed on the 9.6-litre versions, no doubt because they represented more of a continuation of previous practice, yet in the long run this was to be the dominant line of development, admittedly influenced by subsequent dimensional changes. The D3RV synchromesh version was the model that demonstrated just what the key difference between the Mark III and Mark V versions of the Regent amounted to. The A218 engine, D166

gearbox, axles, brakes and most other major units were as used on the 9613S and if the traditional exposed radiator and bonnet were chosen the vehicle looked as well as behaved almost exactly the same as that model. The essential difference lay in the adoption of 4in.-wide road springs in place of the previous 3½in. type, an alteration that enabled the stabiliser used on both axles of the previous provincial model to be eliminated. This was a worthwhile gain as it was beginning to be found that the stabiliser could induce serious cracks in the frame; ultimately some serviceable Mark III buses had their lives shortened by the cost of repairing such failures, if judged uneconomic on a vehicle getting towards the end of its planned life.

The 4in. springs, used on the MD3RV as well as the heavier models, could be recognised from the front on an exposed-radiator model, as the dumb-irons were widened to suit. The MD-series chassis were also readily identifiable by the smaller, 10.00-20, front tyres.

The D2RA model replaced the 9613E but its epicyclic gearbox was not of the preselective type, being of the direct-acting type with electro-pneumatic control, the driver moving a switch unit on the steering column which caused the appropriate gear to be engaged by air pressure, the pedal being eliminated. This system was christened Monocontrol by AEC and was also available slightly later as a fully-automatic system, given the even more awkward name Automonocontrol. The direct-acting epicyclic gearbox was sometimes called semi-automatic, being based on a design of Self-Changing Gears Ltd

and, in essentials, similar to Leyland's Pneumocyclic unit of the same period.

The two 1954 Show vehicles had originally been issued with chassis numbers U168623 and U168627, both having chassis built in AEC's experimental department, but were subsequently given the numbers MD3RV001 and MD3RV002. The first of these was initially given Crossley badges for display purposes (and the chassis quoted as CMD3RV001) but this was simply part of the ACV group's curious Showtime policy and it later became an AEC demonstrator, registered 88 CMV. Its unladen weight, 6 tons 9 cwt 3 qr, with Park Royal 61-seat body, was even less than that of 7194H but I remember wondering whether the diminutive-looking engine, less bulky than the 7.7, was really going to be man enough for double-deck work when I looked in the bonnet. The second vehicle, with similar body, went to Walsall Corporation.

Despite the introduction of new standard designs with quite a wide range of optional features, diversity of specification was on the increase. Orders for new buses were becoming harder to obtain as the demand dropped and AEC was faced with a situation not experienced since the late 'thirties. It was decided to offer Gardner engines as an option, as had been done without publicity in those earlier days, and this was taken slightly farther, even being quoted in the sales leaflets, admittedly in small print. Glasgow Corporation decided not only to specify the 6LW 8.4-litre six-cylinder unit but also the combination of vacuum brakes and preselctive gearbox. Glasgow had not been happy with the effect of a heavy-footed driver

Gardner-engined Regents had been built to special order in the pre-war period and this combination reappeared in 1955-56. Glasgow Corporation was the principal user, taking delivery of 75 of a special version of the Regent V with Gardner 6LW and the combination of preselective gearbox and vacuum brakes also not produced since about fifteen years previously. A pressed radiator grille was specified, giving the completed vehicles a rather utilitarian appearance, which was unfortunate as the bodywork was of the shapely traditional Weymann outline, though using a five-bay structure. However, only 26 were actually built by Weymann, the remainder being built by Alexander to Weymann design. They included A313 (FYS 619) on chassis D2RV6G071, being one of those which entered service in 1956, seen here. Glasgow was one of quite a number of operators which allowed the front wheel-nut guard rings to be discarded, with marked adverse effect on the appearance. The five further D2RV6G chassis built for Aberdeen were of identical appearance but had Crossley bodywork of similar outline to the Liverpool vehicle shown opposite, though also with five-bay structure.

using more severe braking than was desirable for the safety of standing passengers and had been experimenting with the use of a stronger return spring on the air brake pedal, but now decided to revert to the vacuum-servo system. This was no problem in itself, but meant that there would be no air-pressure supply to operate the preselective gearbox (itself officially obsolete). Thus there was a revival of the spring-operated preselective unit, not built since 1940, though the unit now produced was officially a variation of the D150, and was operated via the RT-style steering-column mounted preselector control lever.

Such a vehicle involved extensive detail design due to the combinations of units not previously seen together. The engine mounting consisted of a combination of Gardner's link system at the front and AEC's usual ring behind the fluid flywheel at the rear - fortunately the concealed radiator front-end was just long enough to take the lengthy 6LW but the radiator was moved forward within it, only just clearing the grille panel, which was of a plain slotted design. Glasgow took 75 such buses, all 7ft. 6in. wide, which were given their own chassis number series D2RV6G001-075, the first chassis being sufficient of a new model to be assembled in the experimental department. Aberdeen Corporation took a further five to the same specification, and those chassis actually left Southall first, in April 1955.

I was involved with the 'productionising' of the drawings for the Glasgow job and one of my neighbours in the drawing office was busy at the same time on a Liverpool order for 67 Regent V chassis. These were based on a standard model, the D3RV, being the first of that series and thus D3RV001 up, but also had many non-standard detail features, including

Until well into 1956, standard Regent V models were very much in the minority amid the variety of 'specials'. West Bridgford Urban District Council was among the few receiving MD3RV models before the end of 1955, No. 30 (TRR 953) on chassis MD3RV053 being delivered in December. It was one of three with Park Royal bodywork and is seen here leaving the imposing Council House in Nottingham soon after entering service, wintry weather having defeated this small undertaking's usually immaculate turnout.

Liverpool Corporation's specification was based on the newly-introduced D3RV chassis but for the second time an order for that city involved a non-standard front-end. Although based on the standard outline, it differed in numerous details, such as the square-cornered bonnet and mudguard fairing panels as well as the rubber-edged mudguards themselves. Even the grille, though of Glasgow style, was a different pressing because of the absence of the areas for the maker's badges. The Crossley body structure was much as used on earlier batches of Regent III for Liverpool, A139 on chassis D3RV050 being one of 40 of the initial batch of 67 with bodies completed by LCPT, entering service in March 1956.

The second batch of D3RV models, 30 for Nottingham, were quite different, having the Regent III-style exposed radiator. With Park Royal bodywork, they were very like the Holme Delight 8613S model shown on page 50, the absence of the Mark III model's stabiliser in front of the front axle being a key difference. Number 224, a D3RV083 example, was new in March 1956.

The ACV group standard double-decker concept did have a measure of success in the early Regent V period. Western Welsh Omnibus Co Ltd was noteworthy in taking examples of both lowbridge and highbridge versions of the standard Park Royal-bodied product, though unusually also splitting its order in terms of chassis type. The eight lowbridge buses were the earliest examples of the D3RV 9.6-litre chassis to be completed with the 'official' standard front-end, No. 664 (LKG 664) on D3RV107 being the last of this

batch, delivered in March 1956. The fifteen normal-height (highbridge) buses were on the version with A470 (7.6-litre) engine, No. 669 being MD3RV207 and, like the rest of this type, dating from June 1956. Whatever the intentions of the varied specification, both versions are seen in Cardiff on the same route. The lowbridge bus had a step-ring on its front offside wheel, but the difference in wheel and tyre types is readily evident, even so.

the same style of plain slotted grille; later batches for this fleet had a built-up nearside front mudguard. As the first of these entered service in October 1955, Nottingham was putting the first of its initial batch of 30 D3RV models into service (D3RV068 upwards), these having exposed radiators and replacing the cancelled Regent III models mentioned in Chapter Five — indeed they were to the closest possible specification to a Mark III.

It wasn't until almost the end of 1955 that vehicles which could reasonably be described as standard Regent V models began to appear in service, with a batch of 20 of the light MD3RV type for South Wales followed by a similar fleet for Devon General — Oxford also took an initial seven but those had the exposed radiator. For a time, the BET companies generally favoured the MD3RV, though Western Welsh hedged its bets with eight of the heavier D3RV and fifteen MD3RV in 1956 and Hebble stuck to the 9.6-litre engine in deference to its hilly terrain for two vehicles the same year. In most cases they were traditional AEC customers, though Maidstone & District had favoured Bristol (with AEC engines) and then Leyland for double-deckers in the late 'forties and early 'fifties, and East Yorkshire Motor Services Ltd was a new recruit to the ranks of AEC customers. About 300 Regent V models with the AV470 engine were in service by the end of 1956, roughly half being with BET companies.

Municipal operators accounted for most of the others, but some 80, easily the largest single order, were for Leeds

City Transport which specified another variant not originally listed, the MD2RA, combining the AV470 engine with Monocontrol epicyclic transmission and air-pressure brakes, together with exposed-radiator styling. However, it was decided to follow this up by building a demonstrator, MD2RA298, outwardly like the prototype, 88 CMV, but also with Monocontrol transmission. It was registered 159 JHX and painted dark blue and cream with Birmingham City Transport particularly in mind. AEC had never given up the hope of regaining this undertaking as a major customer, despite the fact that only 20 Regents (five in 1937 and the fifteen RT-type in 1947) had been supplied since the days when AEC was Birmingham's principal supplier of buses ended in 1931. It did not succeed in this but 159 JHX may have played a

part in subsequent MD2RA orders for 25 vehicles from Aberdeen in 1957-59. Otherwise, apart from a repeat order for 55 from Leeds and three buses for West Bridgford, the synchromesh version remained dominant.

This was also true of the 9.6-litre version, the D3RV model accounting for all the 160 or so home-market examples that had entered service by the end of 1956, a figure which also gives an indication of the relative popularity of the two engine sizes at that date. There were, however, 50 D2RA export models with 17ft. 6in. wheelbase supplied to Johannesburg, shipped as chassis in two batches that year. These had the 11.3-litre A222 engine, very similar to the A218 but with bore increased to 130 mm, more to compensate for Johannesburg's high altitude than in search for extra power in itself. The main early D3RV

Leeds City Transport continued to favour traditional styling, so its big delivery of 80 MD2RA-type Regent V models with Roe bodywork looked very much like the four-bay Regent III models added to the fleet from 1950, except that the deep 'Pullman' side windows had given way to a more conventional depth. The vehicle shown when ready for delivery in February 1956 is No. 762 (WUA 762). Leeds C.T. continued to specify 7ft. 6in. width and hence the front wheels did not have the marked offset usual on MD models.

East Yorkshire Motor Services Ltd, previously almost exclusively an operator of Leyland buses, was among the more notable of AEC's sales successes in the 'fifties, though only two orders for a total of nineteen Regent models were fulfilled before a switch to Bridgemasters was made. The AV470-engined model with exposed radiator was chosen for the first seventeen and the bodywork on fifteen, dating from November 1956, had the characteristic 'Gothic' roof shape to allow operation through Beverley Bar, as demonstrated in this view of No. 637 (VKH 37) on chassis MD3RV265. Willowbrook obtained the body contract for this batch, its interpretation of the concept borderng on the bizarre. Another of these vehicles, VKH 44, is preserved and has been restored to typical EYMS smartness; the detail view shows the characteristic dumb-iron shape, wider than on a Regent III, to accommodate the 4in.-wide springs.

(Centre) Great Yarmouth Corporation also chose the MD3RV, but with standard front and to 7ft. 6in. width. Massey built the 58-seat body on No. 27 (EX 9827) on chassis MD3RV300, dating from July 1956, one of five similar buses.

(Below right) Eastbourne Corporation also favoured bodywork from the north-west for its batch of seven 56-seat Regent V delivered slightly earlier in the year but stayed with East Lancashire, by then its traditional supplier. The chassis number of No. 55 (DHC 655) was D3RV150 and the comparison with that of the Great Yarmouth bus accurately conveys the more limited sales at that stage of the 9.6-litre model.

(Below) The export Regent V at first retained the 17ft. 6in. wheelbase of its predecessor. Johannesburg's fleet of 50 D2RA chassis of 1956 were also noteworthy for their 11.3-litre engines. Bus Bodies (South Africa) built the bodywork, No. 254 being seen here.

customers were Liverpool and Nottingham, as already mentioned, plus some smaller municipal fleets.

Meanwhile, the Gardner-engine option had moved on to its final stage. Rochdale Corporation ordered 40 D2RA6G 8ft.-wide chassis, with Gardner 6LW engine but, unlike the Glasgow buses, having air brakes. Of these, ten had the Monocontrol gearbox and were thus the only examples of the Gardner Regent V to have the standard form of epicyclic transmission, but the main batch of

thirty had air-operated preselective gearbox as standard on the Regent III, the only home-market Mark V Regents to be so equipped. All had the standard Regent V 'new look' front-end (this being its official name within AEC) and entered service in 1956.

It is noteworthy that AEC officially listed not only the D2RA6G with Monocontrol transmission but also a D2RA5G version with the Gardner 5LW five-cylinder engine, both being available in either 8ft. or 7ft. 6in. width, at the beginning of 1956, but

none of the 5LW version were built. At that date, the drawing office had reverted to using stroke numbers to distinguish variations, so that D3RV/1 was 8ft.-wide and D3RV/2 was 7ft. 6in. wide, in both cases with 'new look' front while D3RV/3 and D3RV/4 were the corresponding models with exposed radiator (simply called 'half cab'), the same sequence being used for other models, save that the Gardner versions were only offered in 'new look' form.

AEC sent three demonstration buses to Birmingham City Transport in the latter part of the 'fifties. The first, 159 JHX, a Regent V on chassis MD2RA298, had the combination of AV470 engine and epicyclic transmission doubtless thought likely to appeal, at first in standard Monocontrol form, later converted to Automonocontrol fully-automatic. The Park Royal 65-seat body incorporated a standard Birmingham front destination display and was painted in dark blue and cream, though more in Newcastle's 1945-48 style than BCT's. Completed in June 1956, it ran in Birmingham service for various periods as shown, but was not retained and was eventually sold to the independent operator King Alfred Motor Services of Winchester in September 1958, whose subsequent double-decker orders went to AEC until 1964.

Liverpool's final variation on 'new look' front-ends was the addition of a built-up housing to accommodate the nearside sidelamp, looking a rather obvious afterthought. The example shown here was A246 (VKB 879) on chassis D3RV201, one of a further batch of 65 D3RV chassis which received bodywork of a four-bay Orion style by Metro-Cammell (or in some cases based on Metro-Cammell frames but completed by the operator) and entered service between November 1956 and September 1957, the latter date marking the end of Liverpool tramway operation. Further batches of 35 and then 25 chassis with similar bodywork entered service in 1957-59, but these were to be Liverpool's last Regents apart from one 30ft. example purchased for comparative trials.

The first 30ft. Regent on chassis LD2RA347 was displayed at the 1956 Commercial Motor Show, though not in what might have been thought its rightful place on either the AEC stand, or that of Park Royal who built the body. It was officially, if temporarily, a 'Crossley' Regent, being displayed on that concern's stand, amid almost negligible publicity, though it had never been near Crossley's works at Stockport. This was a curious decision as the Crossley stand also had the ACV group's star exhibit of that Show, the prototype Bridgemaster low-floor double-decker which had been dveloped by Crossley, even though of AEC/Park Royal basic design. History had the last laugh, for the sales of 30ft. Regents were about 2½ times the 179 Bridgemaster models built in the period up to 1962 when the latter was in production — ultimately, over 1,000 of the 30ft. right-hand Regent models were built. The two Show vehicles both had Monocontrol transmission and this view of SDF 281 with its Crossley nameplates reveals the unladen weight to have been a modest 7 tons 15 cwt.

Chapter eight:
Enter the 30ft. Regent
1956-59

In January 1956, AEC had made its initial plans for Regent V models to suit the Ministry of Transport's proposed increase of maximum length to take two-axle double-deckers to 30ft. There were to be two basic types, each with the A218 9.6-litre engine and 18ft. 6in. wheelbase, the LD2RA, with the Monocontrol epicyclic transmission and basically an extended version of the D2RA 16ft. 4in. wheelbase model, and the LD3RA, with synchromesh gearbox but having air-pressure brakes. AEC, unlike Leyland, decided from the start not to offer 30ft. Regent models with vacuum brakes. A point in common with Leyland, still the most direct rival, was that 7ft. 6in.-wide 30ft. versions were not to be offered, and there was to be a choice of the AEC version of the 'new look' front-

end or the traditional Mark III style front with exposed radiator, the respective drawing office variation suffix codes being LD2RA/1 and LD2RA/2 or LD3RA/1 and LD3RA/2.

By 1st July, when the revised regulations came into force, the specification had been slightly revised, the wheelbase length becoming 18ft. 7in. However, two LD2RA chassis were already in hand for display, complete with 73-seat Park Royal bodywork, at that year's Commercial Motor Show and these retained the 18ft. 6in. dimension. Numerically the first 30ft. Regent was LD2RA347, for the independent operator F. C. Cottrell of Mitcheldean, Gloucestershire, registered SDF 281, which was displayed on the Crossley stand and accordingly carried Crossley badges,

replaced by AEC before the vehicle was delivered. The other bus, very similar apart from having a detachable top cover, was on 'neighbouring' chassis LD2RA348 (both being numbered in the same series as 27ft. 'D' models which continued unchanged) and was Western Welsh No. 680 (MUH 680).

Subsequent 30ft. Regent V models had the 18ft. 7in. wheelbase, but over a year passed before they began to take the road in any quantity, among the first production examples to enter service being three for Mayne of Manchester, again with Park Royal bodywork, in July 1957, though 20 for Rhondda Transport Ltd had lower chassis numbers, LD3RA353-372, suggesting that they were ordered by about the end of 1956. These latter did not enter service until January 1958,

possibly because they had forward-entrance bodywork, as vehicles with the doorway just behind the front axle were now generally called. This was a revival of an idea which had been quite popular in the 'thirties, when Regents with bodywork of this layout had been built for quite a number of important operators (as described in volume No. 7 of this series) but had been generally out of favour for fifteen years or so. Its revival was related to general use of the front-entrance layout on underfloor-engined single-deckers and also as a reaction to the prototype Leyland Atlantean, also with entrance at the extreme front, displayed at the 1956 Show. Even though there was no suggestion at that stage of eliminating the conductor, the idea of making the

driver more directly responsible for supervising passenger entry and exit was growing in favour.

The Rhondda vehicles had Weymann bodywork based on the Orion design and ten almost identical vehicles but bodied by MCW's other 'partner', Metro-Cammell, were supplied to Yorkshire (Woollen District) the same month, and for several years such vehicles were to be standard in other BET fleets, either long-established AEC customers like Rhondda itself or South Wales and to a slightly less historic degree Hebble, or new convert Yorkshire (WD).

The ACV group's own bodybuilder, Park Royal, did not take part in this revival of interest in the forward-entrance double-decker until later in

The other 1956 Show example of the 30ft. Regent V was for Western Welsh and though in general similar to the Cottrell vehicle, its Park Royal body was noteworthy in having a detachable top to the upper-deck, made in glass-fibre reinforced plastics, then a relatively novel material. Number 680, on chassis LS2RA348, seen in Cardiff some years later, was destined to remain a 'one-off', subsequent Western Welsh double-deck orders being 20 Bridgemasters and then in 1960-62, some 66 Leyland Atlantean, though one final batch of ten 27ft. mediumweight Regents was to follow in 1963.

1958, perhaps because it was involved, with Crossley, in the development of the Bridgemaster integral-construction low-floor double-decker which added a

Utilitarian though it may have looked, this Weymann-bodied 70-seat LD3RA-type Regent V belonged to a batch that was an important trend-setter. What is now called the forward-entrance layout had been out of fashion, with only a couple of exceptions, for nearly two decades but was suddenly 'in' again from the late 'fifties. The MCW Orion standard was produced in this form, complete with angled bulkhead window, to give the driver greater ability to supervise loading, though one-man operation of double-deckers was to remain illegal for another eight years. Rhondda Transport took the 20 vehicles to which No. 426 (VTX 426) on chassis LD3RA354 belonged early in 1958, but within a few months both Weymann and Metro-Cammell were supplying similarly-bodied Regents to several other BET companies and municipalities.

The demand for 27ft. Regents was virtually unaffected by the availability of the 30ft. version in 1957, and in many cases continued much longer. St. Helens Corporation took delivery of six AV470-engined synchromesh models, including H138 (GDJ 438) on chassis MD3RV435 seen here, in August 1957. They had 61-seat bodywork to Orion specification by Weymann, differing in almost every aspect of specification and appearance but the rear wheel disc from the RT-type buses which had been St. Helens' standard in 1950-52. The following year, 24 more Regent V were supplied but on the D3RV chassis with 9.6-litre engine, though the MD3RV was again favoured for eight in 1959. Most of these had similar Weymann bodywork but it was even more remarkable that three buses delivered as late as 1967 were of similar pattern, though in that case on AV590-engined chassis.

After the flurry of interest in Gardner-engined Regents in 1955-56, all three customers subsequently reverted to AEC-engined models. Aberdeen Corporation chose the MD2RA chassis with AV470 engine and Monocontrol semi-automatic gearbox, the first five to arrive in November-December 1957 having Park Royal bodywork and thus somewhat resembling the demonstrator 159 JHX, though seating some 66 passengers, the maximum practicable on a conventional 27ft. front-engined double-decker — No. 250 (KRS 250) seen here, was on chassis MD2RA466. Fifteen more with Metro-Cammell bodywork followed in 1958 and a final five bodied by Alexander in 1959. In the early 'sixties it was found that the AV470 engines were requiring frequent repair and five of the MD2RA models were converted with Gardner 6LW engines, partly to create a float of spare units for overhaul.

third disparate strand to AEC's involvement with double-deckers. Despite its name, it had little in common with the Routemaster beyond the fact that both were integral and had independent front suspension, and even less with the Regent, apart from parts of the running gear, and in some ways could be seen as the ACV group's answer to the Bristol-ECW Lodekka design in which the Managing Director of AEC, A. J. Romer, had been closely involved prior to his move to Southall; there was widespread interest in the low-floor idea at the time. The prototype

Bridgemaster, hastily extended from 27ft. to 30ft long, had appeared on the Crossley stand at the 1956 Show and the group had then been involved in an expensive major redesign to change the structure from aluminium alloy to steel and a disruptive removal of production of this model to Park Royal, as Crossley's works was to be closed.

Meanwhile, with both Routemaster and Bridgemaster contributing no more than a handful of prototypes to AEC's output, the Regent soldiered on as the only double-decker model to be earning the firm some money. Even so, output was well down from the halcyon

days of the Mark III, and even the fairly modest surge of demand which followed the introduction of the Mark V range was not maintained. In terms of registrations, the peak year for the Regent V was 1956, when about 450 examples entered service in Britain, of which more than half were of the lighter MD3RV or MD2RA types, plus 30 exported to Johannesburg. The average for the Regent III had been around 1,000 per year, with London Transport alone putting over that number of RT models on the road in its peak year, 1950.

The annual totals of Regent models

Sales of new double-deckers to independent operators in the 'fifties rarely amounted to sizeable numbers of vehicles, but AEC secured its fair share. Osborne & Sons of Tollesbury, Essex, had been an AEC customer intermittently since 1931, when the first of several Regal coaches was purchased and its first Regent had been a 9612A-type in 1950. In May 1957, this Regent V entered service, noteworthy in having the combination of 9.6-litre engine and Monocontrol semi-automatic transmission not often associated with lowbridge bodywork, the latter being built by Park Royal and seating 59. It was given the fleet number 1 and was mounted on chassis number D2RA380. Osborne's was about to build up quite a fleet of AEC double-deckers, five ex-London Transport RT-type buses being bought at intervals between 1958 and 1965 and three former AEC demonstrators (two Bridgemaster and a Renown), regularly to be seen on its services to Colchester.

entering service in Britain dropped to around the 175 mark by 1958 and the figure for right-hand drive models in general remained steady at about that figure until 1961, thanks to export orders. As will be told in more detail in Chapter Nine, left-hand export models improved the overall picture considerably, but even so total Regent output for all versions over the 1958-61 period averaged a little over 300 chassis annually, or roughly half Leyland's output of Titan models. In the Regent III era, the two firms had been rivals for the leading place among builders of double-deckers and AEC was in front at times, especially when RT output for London Transport was at its peak. On the other hand, AEC's strength among home-market bus business at this period was concentrated on the very popular Reliance single-decker.

The 'heavy' models became much more numerous from 1957-58 and this was only partly related to the addition of the 30ft. versions as demand for the MD-series chassis dwindled, mainly becoming concentrated on smaller municipal fleets. Other operators in this category favoured the 9.6-litre chassis but tended to continue with the 27ft. overall length, sometimes even retaining 7ft. 6in. width, as at Ipswich, Colchester and Douglas. A single vehicle of these dimensions, D3RV373, supplied to Darwen Corporation in 1957 as No. 17 (434 BTE) was noteworthy as being ordered and delivered as a Crossley Regent V, a unique combination if considered on a permanent basis, unlike several Commercial Motor Show exhibits of the 'fifties temporarily thus badged. Darwen had been a purchaser of 'genuine' Crossley double-deckers in

1949-52 and the vehicle in question was accompanied by three Crossley Reliance single-deckers. St. Helens was another unusual case for six MD3RV placed in service in 1957, followed by 24 D3RV in 1958 and then eight more MD3RV in 1959, all being 27ft.-long.

Most of the larger early orders for the 30ft. models went to established AEC customers, but in addition to Yorkshire (Woollen District), already mentioned, the East Kent Road Car Co Ltd was another BET company which had been introduced to AEC vehicles by the Reliance single-deckers after a long history of favouring other makes. The first of its initial batch of 40 examples was exhibited at the 1958 Commercial Motor Show and was noteworthy as the first example of the Regent V to have a new design of engine.

Barton Transport Ltd's much larger fleet included only a few AEC buses until the mid-'fifties, when the Reliance was favoured as a basis for most new single-decker purchases. The first two Regent V models, delivered in September 1957, arrived at a time when Barton had temporarily abandoned its inclination to rather elaborate double-deck body designs. Curiously, this firm's traditional favour for the forward-entrance layout was also dropped just as it was coming back into more general favour. The Northern Counties 67-seat lowbridge bodywork on these two 30ft. buses was very similar to that being supplied to Western SMT on Leyland PD3 chassis. Number 784 (XAL 784) on chassis LD3RA455 has survived, looking very much as it did when new, being seen here at the 1986 AEC Society rally at Derby.

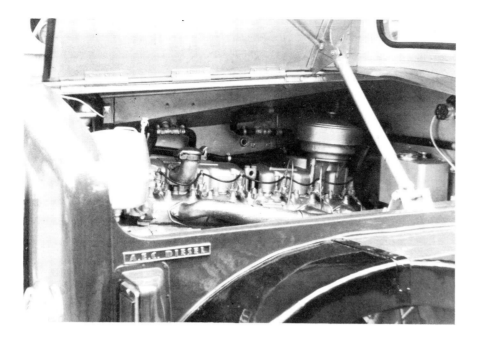

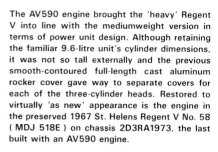

The AV590 engine brought the 'heavy' Regent V into line with the mediumweight version in terms of power unit design. Although retaining the familiar 9.6-litre unit's cylinder dimensions, it was not so tall externally and the previous smooth-contoured full-length cast aluminum rocker cover gave way to separate covers for each of the three-cylinder heads. Restored to virtually 'as new' appearance is the engine in the preserved 1967 St. Helens Regent V No. 58 (MDJ 518E) on chassis 2D3RA1973, the last built with an AV590 engine.

The first operator to receive AV590-powered Regent models was the East Kent Road Car Co Ltd, which placed 40 of the new 2LD3RA model in service in 1958-59. The 72-seat bodywork was of the full-fronted forward-entrance type already in use by some other BET companies though this was the first Regent V version and the first from Park Royal — the appearance, though imposing, was almost literally flat-fronted, lacking the subtlety of half-cab versions of basically similar design. Seen when ready for delivery early in 1959 is PFN 845, on chassis 2LD3RA546, while PFN 868 is seen in service the following summer.

This was the AV590 and had the same cylinder dimensions and hence 9.6-litre capacity as the A218 but differed from it in having similar construction to the AV470 used in MD-series Regents. The combined cylinder block and crankcase simplified the design and in itself was probably beneficial. More controversial was the adoption of the same wet-liner internal construction, which requires suitable arrangements for effectively sealing the cooling water, directly in contact with each liner. The AV470 and its horizontal equivalent, the AH470, standard in the Reliance single-decker, had already earned a reputation for cylinder head gasket failure if worked hard, and this may partly account for the fall-off in interest for the MD-series Regent models. The AV590 was advertised as developing up to 140 bhp for some applications but for the Regent V was kept down to 128 bhp at

1,800 rpm — barely more than the older 9.6-litre's traditional 125 bhp.

The AV590-engined models were given a prefix '2' to the chassis numbers — in effect a revival of the fourth figure in the previous system and thus the East Kent 1958 Show vehicle had chassis number 2LD3RA544, the batch continuing to 2LD3RA583, these entering service in 1959. Yorkshire (Woollen District)'s second batch of Regents, with DHD registration numbers, was also of this type and had rather earlier numbers 2LD3RA478-492, but these did not enter service until January 1959. On the other hand, not only the chassis with intervening numbers, which had entered service in 1958, but also a subsequent delivery of fifteen LD2RA for Bradford with PKY registrations placed in service in May-July 1959, some 60 vehicles on the 17ft. 6in. wheelbase D2RA type chassis for

Johannesburg plus smaller orders for Rochdale and Colchester with chassis numbers up to D3RV665, plus one slightly higher-numbered batch for Ipswich, D2RA719-722, retained the earlier engine and therefore did not have the prefix number. The home-market A218-engined vehicles in question were all in service by the summer of 1959 and the switch-over was thus quite rapid, though as will be explained later the left-hand models continued to use the old-series engines well into the 'sixties.

At almost the same time, it was decided to drop the L prefix signifying the 18ft. 7in. wheelbase length. It was argued that other AEC models, goods and passenger, were offered with alternative wheelbases without such distinction but the decision contrasted with Leyland's use of the completely different PD3 series of type numbers to distinguish its 30ft. range from the

As one door opened, another closed. Similar in basic design to the buses that introduced the AEC Regent to an important new customer at East Kent, the vehicle shown above proved to be the final chapter in Liverpool Corporation's association with the model, which had been continuous, apart from the war period, since 1935. Liverpool decided to carry out comparative tests, using three vehicles with 'experimental' E-prefix fleet numbers and E1, with AV590 engine and Monocontrol semi-automatic transmission, received 72-seat Park Royal bodywork similar in essentials to the East Kent batch but incorporating numerous detail differences, such as the fixed windscreens (newly permissible under a change in regulations) and top-hinged nearside cab

emergency exit in which the route number was displayed. It was delivered in June 1959 but the chassis number, 2DRA374, and other evidence suggests that the origins of the chassis may have gone back a couple of years earlier — some of Liverpool's 16ft. 4in. Regents placed in service in 1957-58 had slightly higher sales order and chassis numbers. Note the perforated radiator grille introduced at 1958 Show time — the small inclined 'Regent' title in the offside panel was almost a revival of Mark II practice. The outcome of the trials was Liverpool's decision to buy Leyland Atlantean rear-engined buses for future orders.

Hebble Motor Services Ltd had run an exclusively Regent-based double-deck fleet from 1953, a situation which continued until 1966. Rebuilding of the company's garage made it possible to use highbridge vehicles from 1957 and forward-entrance 71-seat MCW Orion-style 30ft. Regent V models were added to the fleet in 1958 (two vehicles), 1959 (four) and 1960 (two), the last-mentioned with bodies built by Metro-Cammell instead of Weymann as previously. Number 309 (LJX 200) on chassis 2D3RA729 of the 1959 batch is seen looking rather shabby in later years in Bradford bus station — it was to be one of the vehicles still in the fleet when most of Hebble's bus operations were taken over by Halifax Joint Omnibus Committee in 1971.

PD2. The last L-prefix chassis were in fact the Bradford vehicles mentioned above, LD2RA584-598, the next 18ft. 7in. wheelbase chassis being 2D3RA666 for South Wales, which entered service in March 1959.

More significantly, the end of an era was signalled by Leeds City Transport's first 2D2RA buses, fourteen 18ft. 7in. wheelbase models, 2D2RA731-744, supplied in May-June 1960, for they were the last to have the traditional Regent III-style radiator. It was perhaps ironic that they had Metro-Cammell Orion bodywork after the long tradition, including a succession of Earls Court Show models, of the Leeds-Regent-Roe combination; AEC had decided to withdraw this option, for which there was now little demand.

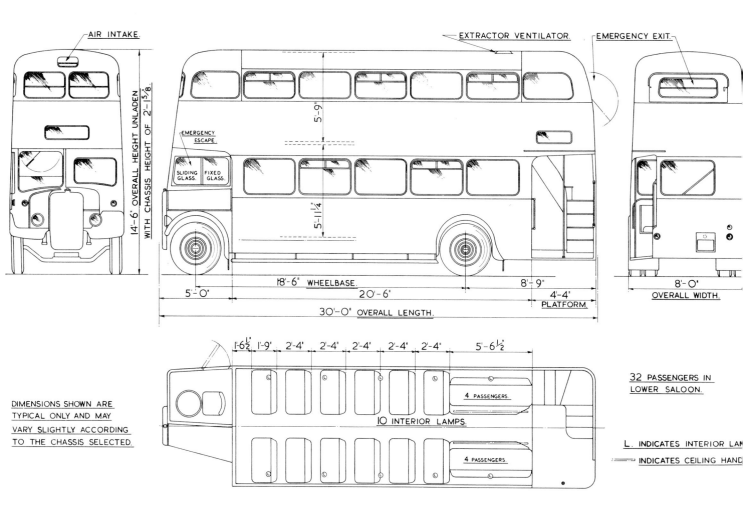

AIR INTAKE.

14'-6" OVERALL HEIGHT UNLADEN WITH CHASSIS HEIGHT OF 2'-1⅝"

EXTRACTOR VENTILATOR.

EMERGENCY EXIT.

EMERGENCY ESCAPE.

SLIDING GLASS. FIXED GLASS.

5'-9"

5'-11¼"

18'-6" WHEELBASE.

5'-0"

20'-6"

8'-9"

4'-4" PLATFORM.

30'-0" OVERALL LENGTH.

8'-0" OVERALL WIDTH.

DIMENSIONS SHOWN ARE TYPICAL ONLY AND MAY VARY SLIGHTLY ACCORDING TO THE CHASSIS SELECTED.

1'-6½" 1'-9" 2'-4" 2'-4" 2'-4" 2'-4" 2'-4" 5'-6½"

4 PASSENGERS.

10 INTERIOR LAMPS.

4 PASSENGERS.

32 PASSENGERS IN LOWER SALOON.

L. INDICATES INTERIOR LAMP

INDICATES CEILING HAND

This drawing, issued by MCW and reproduced to 4mm scale, is clearly based on a 30ft.-long Regent V in exposed-radiator form, even though the radiator detail is omitted in the front elevation to allow it to be used to represent other chassis models. The wheelbase length of 18ft. 6in. suggests that it was originally issued in the 1956 period when this had been the wheelbase of the LD2RA and LD3RA as originally designed. As it turned out, however, the only vehicles built which broadly conformed to this drawing were the batch of 2D2RA 18ft. 7in.-wheelbase models for Leeds City Transport which had the distinction of being the last exposed-radiator Regent models built and the only 30ft.-long Regents with the traditional style of front-end. In that case the bodies were built by Metro-Cammell and seated 71, entering service as Leeds 910-923 in May-June 1960.

Garelochhead Coach Services Ltd took delivery of this AV470-engined Regent V in August 1959. It was the second of two with Alexander 65-seat rear-entrance bodywork for this fleet, though the previous one, HSN 485, had been delivered just over a year earlier. It had the chassis number MD3RV171 while the vehicle shown, JSN 584, was MD3RV170, both evidently instances of gap-filling in the chassis number series of the kind familiar in the Regent III period but rare by that date — other vehicles of the 1958-59 period having numbers nearer 500 or so. Garelochhead continued to be a regular purchaser of mediumweight Regents, buying single examples with Northern Counties forward-entrance bodywork in 1964/5/6, ending with the vehicle bearing the final number, 2MD3RA645 in 1968, registered MSN 863G.

By the 'sixties, the forward-entrance layout had become the majority choice. Sheffield's first examples on Regent chassis arrived in 1963, including this example, one of nine for the Joint Committee 'B' fleet with Park Royal 70-seat bodywork of the Orion-like style by then current. Number 1359 (359 EWE) was on chassis 2D2RA1266 — in addition to the change of entrance position, Sheffield had switched back to epicyclic transmission, by then of the semi-automatic Monocontrol type, of course. This was one of several major fleets where the rear-engined double-decker already had a firm foothold; the last Sheffield Regents were purchased in 1964.

Chapter nine:
Regents of the 'sixties

By 1960 there was increasing demand for 30ft. double-deckers, Sheffield making the switch with 46 2D3RA models for its Corporation and Joint Committee fleets, some of which were needed for the final stage of that city's tram replacement programme. Halifax was another Yorkshire municipality to adopt this model for its first 30ft. buses, fourteen vehicles which also marked a return to AEC after Daimler and Leyland vehicles had been favoured in the middle to late 'fifties. Another but larger case of a return to the AEC fold after an admittedly shorter absence, from 1956, was Glasgow, although some 300 Leyland and 150 Daimler double-deckers had been placed in service in the interim, again as part of a major tramway replacement. In 1960-61, 89 Regent 2D2RA models of the 18ft. 7in. wheelbase type entered service, these being noteworthy for having Alexander forward-entrance bodywork, one of the

few instances of buses of this layout entering service in one of the largest city fleets. However, this was to be a swan song, as no further Regents were to be added to the Glasgow fleet, which had been a large-scale operator of successive versions of the model going back to 1930.

'Final' batches of Regent models were beginning to occur in other fleets where they had long been familiar, and even though no-one knew that this was to be so at the time, trends were not in favour of a revival. In Glasgow, the rear-engined double-decker was set to take over, following experiments with an early production Leyland Atlantean. At City of Oxford Motor Services Ltd, it was decided to adopt low-floor models as standard and though these were to be mostly AEC Bridgemaster and, later, Renown models, it meant the end of the road for new Regents after a similar 30-year spell. Oxford had been one of the

minority of companies which returned to the light MD3RV model after one batch of LD3RA in 1958, latterly having adopted the standard 'new look' front-end, and the final batches taken into stock respectively at the beginning and end of 1960 were ten with Willowbrook and five with East Lancashire bodywork, forward-entrance in both cases. It was noteworthy that five Dennis Loline buses purchased in 1961 were fitted with AEC AV470 engines, clearly indicating that this unit had proved satisfactory in this operator's circumstances.

Even so, it was the larger-engined model that was more widely favoured, its chassis number series having passed the 1000 mark during 1961 when the MD series had yet to pass 550. By the end of that year, regular customers such as Hebble, Rhondda and South Wales had progressed to 2D3RA models of 18ft. 7in. wheelbase, Ipswich

Almost the last in a long line of Regents supplied to City of Oxford Motor Services Ltd were ten 27ft. models dating from January 1960 on the AV470-engined chassis with forward-entrance 83-seat bodywork by Willowbrook, exemplified here by No. 984 (984 HFC) on chassis MD3RV487. The bodies had the frameless front dome construction widely favoured at the time, with its inevitable wide corner pillars, but were rather better proportioned than many other body designs of the period, the effect being helped by Oxford's traditional livery style. A low bridge had long plagued this operator and, although highbridge buses had been used where possible, the concept of a low-floor double-decker led to a switch to the Bridgemaster and then Renown.

and West Bridgford had 2D2RA Monocontrol 16ft. 4in. batches while Eastbourne and St. Helens had 2D3RV synchromesh vacuum-braked batches in service. Relative newcomers such as East Kent and Barton Transport, the latter having taken a couple of LD3RA in 1957, had come back for 18ft. 7in. 2D3RA models and the long-wheelbase Monocontrol 2D2RA had attracted orders from Bradford, Walsall and Huddersfield.

Several of these operators took further batches of the same models in 1962, though Bradford switched from the Monocontrol 2D2RA to the synchromesh 2D3RA for ten vehicles that year and some 90 further buses in 1963-64, a somewhat surprising move at that date for a municipal fleet that had generally favoured epicyclic transmission since the mid-thirties, except when the final tramway replacement fleet was augmented by Leylands and a few Crossleys in 1949-50. Oddly enough, Sheffield went the opposite way with a total of 31 2D2RA in 1963-64, perhaps influenced by Leyland Atlantean models with semi-automatic transmission then in the fleet, after favouring synchromesh AEC models since 1953.

Even more surprising was Southampton Corporation's re-appearance in the lists of AEC Regent purchasers after an interval of some 32 years, during which Leyland and Guy buses had been favoured. The first batch in 1962 were ten 16ft. 4in.-wheelbase chassis, 2D3RA1051-59, the option of air brakes on the short-wheelbase synchromesh version having been added the previous year. These first examples had oddly-proportioned Park Royal bodywork partly based on components intended for the Bridgemaster, but 30 more delivered in two batches in 1963-65 had more traditional East Lancashire bodies, in all cases with the high seating capacity for a 27ft.-long model of 66. Southampton was destined to be an important Regent customer in the final phase of production.

An important event in 1963 was the building of 30 buses for the Kowloon Motor Bus Co (1933) Ltd, based in the mainland New Territories area of Hong Kong. Major expansion of Hong Kong's bus fleets was getting under way and the Kowloon concern had to cope with the supply of public transport for vast satellite townships. Accordingly a special version of the 2D2RA model was produced, with 21ft. 6in. wheelbase to allow an overall length of over 34ft. and powered by the AV690 engine, basically similar to the standard AV590 but of 11.3-litre capacity and developing 154 bhp at 1,800 rpm. An order was placed for 110 chassis, to be delivered in batches of 30, 40 and 40 in the period up to 1965. A further 100 were subsequently ordered, delivered in 1965-66. The two-doorway bodywork was built by the operator, using framing supplied by Metal Sections Ltd of Oldbury, and was designed to carry up to 118 passengers, including 78 seated.

Another export market for right-hand Regent models was West

East Kent abandoned the full-fronted body style after the one batch dating from 1958-59 and the next batch of sixteen vehicles to emerge from Park Royal for this operator were of the much more austere design which was to remain standard for succeeding deliveries. This view of WFN 834 on chassis 2D3RA994 about to emerge from the bodybuilder's finishing shop prior to delivery in August 1961 also shows the wider spacing of the front springs resulting from the parallel-sided frame made possible by standardising on 8ft. overall width.

Staff transport for the employees of the United Kingdom Atomic Energy Authority at Harwell and Aldermaston had been provided by a fleet of ex-London Transport RT-type buses, but it was decided to purchase eleven new Regent V models with 73-seat forward-entrance Park Royal bodywork, all being delivered in March 1962. They were painted in a not unattractive blue and light grey livery, though the unbroken expanse of blue emphasised the height of the upper-deck waistrail. Park Royal's standard double-deck body design of that era had much in common with the contemporary Bridgemaster and the 'Meccano-set' approach made a remarkable contrast to the coachbuilding subtleties that had been usual a decade earlier. The 'destination' display on 242 AJB, on chassis 2D3RA1111, refers to the Atomic Energy Research Establishment, Harwell.

BY 1962, rear-entrance double-deckers were rarely purchased for company fleets, but Devon General's 949 (949 HTT) on chassis MD3RV564 was the last of a batch of seven with 59-seat Weymann Orion bodywork delivered in May of that year to join some earlier similar buses for use on Exeter city services, then jointly operated with the muncipal fleet which was continuing to purchase Leyland PD2 models of similar layout. Note the illuminated advertisement panel on the upper deck, a feature then quite common on new vehicles.

Pakistan Road Transport Corporation, to which a dozen 2D3RA chassis with Weymann bodywork were supplied in 1961, followed by seventeen with Metro-Cammell bodies in 1962 and 37 in 1963, the latter understood to have been bodied locally. These export orders helped to build up the numbers, the annual total of D-series 'heavyweight' right-hand Regent V models placed in service or shipped rising above 200 for the first time in 1963, the total of 228 happening to coincide with a minor resurgence of interest in the MD mediumweight series, of which 38 entered service.

The main reason for this was a decision by several of the BET companies to place further batches of 27ft.-long double-deckers in service. This had begun to show up as a

significant factor in 1962, when the Rhondda, Hebble and Devon General concerns between them purchased fourteen of the MD3RV type, these chassis, MD3RV550-564 being the only examples of the type delivered that year. The seven for Devon General were unusual among BET vehicles at that date in having rear-entrance bodywork, chosen to operate alongside similar buses dating from 1958 on Exeter city services. Bigger orders followed in 1963, Devon General taking a further sixteen MD3RV chassis, this time with forward-entrance bodywork. Rhondda took a further ten but these and a similar number for Western Welsh being on the newly-introduced 2MD3RA chassis. This had air-pressure brakes in conjunction with the synchromesh gearbox, the air system

being of the split-circuit type as had been standard on air-braked D-series models since the late 'fifties.

The Regent range was now simplified by the deletion of the vacuum-braked models and the 7ft. 6in. width option, the last medium-weight 7ft. 6in. buses having been supplied to Doncaster in January 1960, apart from a special Leeds Welfare Department single-decker in June of that year, while the last D-series examples were for Colchester and Ipswich in 1959. The MD2RA series was also no longer listed. The first of the final variant of the mediumweight Regent V was 2MD3RA582, Western Welsh 703 (703 CUH) and all higher-numbered examples of this range were of this type except for MD3RV592-593, Lowestoft Corporation 7 and 8 (917-

Barton Transport Ltd had reverted both to the forward-entrance lowbridge layout and its tradition of having double-deckers with a touch of glamour about them. Northern Counties was now well established as supplier of this firm's double-deck bodywork and this firm, too, had never succumbed to the box-on-wheels philosophy. So the appearance of a completely fresh approach to double-deck styling on four Regent V models claimed to be the first double-deckers with curved-glass windscreens in 1960 was in character for both

Barton and Northern Counties. The AEC grille was retained but the rest of the front-end design, still modern-looking today, was the work of the bodybuilder, and one cannot help but wonder what praise might have been lavished on it, had it been the work of one of the Italian designers then so fashionable in the automobile world. The vehicle shown, 962 (962 PRR) on chassis 2D3RA1240, was one of a further batch of six dating from May 1963.

918 NRT) which were placed in service in January 1963 and were numerically the last MD3RV models though the sixteen Devon General examples entered service a few months later, mainly in June 1963. The same month the last vacuum-braked Regents of all, on chassis 2D3RV1261-1265, arrived in the Eastbourne Corporation fleet as 66-70 (KHC 366-370). Oddly Eastbourne was also to have the last Leyland Titans to be built with vacuum

brakes, though that was not until 1967.

The mild boom in demand for the Regent reached its peak in 1964, the best year for deliveries and shipments since 1958. The export demand helped greatly, but sizeable fleets went to regular customers — South Wales and East Kent (20 of the 2D3RA type apiece), Leeds (fifteen 2D2RA followed by 20 more delivered in the winter of 1964-65, though these were to be the last for this fleet which had

continuously favoured Regent models with epicyclic gearboxes since 1934), in addition to vehicles for Bradford, Sheffield and Southampton already mentioned and several smaller orders.

By 1965 the peak was over and had it not been for 65 of the Kowloon ultra-long 2D2RA chassis, this would have been quite a thin year, though South Wales came back for 21 more 2D3RA, this time of 16ft. 4in. wheelbase type. The mediumweight Regent 2MD3RA

Northern Counties also maintained high standards of appearance and finish in more traditional style of bodywork as confirmed the same month by the delivery of this 27ft. Regent V for Western Welsh, the last of ten with 65-seat forward-entrance highbridge bodywork by this builder. They were based on the newly-introduced version of the AV470-engined model with split-circuit air-pressure brakes, No. 712 (712 CUH) seen here in Cardiff being on chassis 2MD3RA591.

Another bodybuilder with a long history of stylish design, Charles H. Roe Ltd, was by the 'sixties building both traditional and what might unkindly be called tin-box products. The Grimsby & Cleethorpes Transport Joint Committee (which had merged the former separate Grimsby and Cleethorpes undertakings in the 'fifties) chose the former style, though the body layout, with forward entrance, had fallen into line with the more usual contemporary practice. Seen here is No. 61 (VJV 503), one of four Regent V with Monocontrol transmission delivered in July 1963. The chassis number, 2D2RA1419, conveys how far the emphasis had swung over to the heavyweight chassis by that date, largely as in this case related to the 30ft. length. The vehicle with similar bodywork on the left of the picture is a Daimler CVG6.

These two pictures taken at the Manchester terminus of A. Mayne & Son Ltd's old-established route to Droylsden illustrate an example of what could almost be described as a revolt against the austere approach to body design. Mayne's had taken three early 30ft. Regent V buses with Park Royal bodywork very like that shown on page 62, and ordered a further three for delivery in 1961. The rear-entrance layout and 73-seat capacity were as on the earlier vehicles, but the design was at just about Park Royal's most utilitarian, as shown by 6972 ND on chassis 2D3RA1095, placed in service in December 1961. When a further two buses of similar general character were wanted two years later, the body order went to Neepsend Coachworks Ltd of Sheffield, another of East Lancashire Coachbuilders' associate concerns. The resulting bodies were to East Lancs design and more traditional character. The pair, 8859 and 8860 VR, on chassis 2D3RA1513 and '1514 were placed in service in January 1964 and are seen together, over sixteen years later, in June 1980.

Bedwas & Machen Urban District Council had been a regular, if small-scale, purchaser of AEC Regent models since 1952, when the vehicle shown on page 43 was added to the fleet. Subsequent examples were all Regent V mediumweight models, one being added to the fleet in 1956, 1957, 1959, 1961 and finally in 1964, when the vehicle shown, BWO 585B on an air-braked chassis, 2MD3RA609, was delivered in September as No. 8, directly

replacing the 1952 Regent III of the same number. The 59-seat lowbridge bodywork was by Massey Bros of Wigan, also responsible for the bodywork on the three previous examples. In the local government reorganisation of 1974 this fleet was absorbed by the newly-formed Rhymney Valley District Council and the fleet number 92 allocated to this vehicle though it at first continued to run in original livery, as shown.

Another consistent Regent buyer was Felix Motors Ltd of Hatfield, near Doncaster, Roe bodywork being generally favoured from the first example supplied new in 1938. Seen here is the last of a total of fourteen, including one second-hand example, purchased over the years. Number 47, (KYG 313D) on chassis 2D3RA1807, was also the last of four 30ft. examples supplied in the 'sixties and having 73-seat rear-entrance Roe bodywork, this one dating from April 1966.

took on quite a Welsh flavour too, as apart from a final half dozen for Devon General, three individual vehicles for Garelochhead Coach Services and one for York Pullman, all the final 50 examples went to operators in the principality. Pontypridd Urban District Council took two in 1965, two in 1966, seven in 1967 and a final two registered in 1969. Rhondda took twelve more in 1965 and five in 1966, while Bedwas & Machen UDC put one on the road in 1964.

Meanwhile the heavier version had one fnal design change. A new 11.3-litre engine, the AV691, had been introduced early in 1966. This had the same 130 mm bore and 142 mm stroke as the AV690 and continued to be of monobloc construction and generally similar design but reverted to dry cylinder liners, eliminating the sealing and related gasket problems which had never been completely eradicated from the previous AV-series wet liner engines. The new design was not being made in 9.6-litre size, the main

demand for goods models now being for a more powerful unit, but for bus work it was quite drastically derated to the same 128 bhp output at 1,800 rpm as had been standard with the AV590 — in other applications it could develop over 200 bhp.

The chassis was given the new designation 3D2RA or 3D3RA when fitted with this engine, and the first such chassis 3D2RA1842 was built for Southampton Corporation in February 1966. That undertaking had ordered 30 of the 18ft. 7in. wheelbase chassis and they entered service with a lengthened version of the East Lancashire body design used on the previous examples between May 1966 and December 1967. Orders for 2D-series models entered service with several fleets during much the same period, including final batches for Devon General (five 2D3RA 16ft. 4in. models, a type also again favoured by South Wales for its final eighteen). East Kent took 30 of the 18ft. 7in. version of this model in 1966, and there were smaller orders for

Devon General's final batch of Regents were of interest in several respects. They were of the shorter, 16ft. 4in. wheelbase type, yet unlike previous Regent V models of similar dimensions in this fleet were 9.6-litre buses of type 2D3RA. The 59-seat forward-entrance bodywork could truly be said to be of Metro-Cammell Weymann construction, being assembled at Metro-Cammell from some of the last sets of parts produced by the Weymann works before it closed. The vehicle shown, No. 521 (EOD 521D) on chassis 2D3RA1802 was the first of the batch, dating from July 1966.

Park Royal's painters could still turn out good quality work, as demonstrated by GJG 746D, one of 30 further 72-seat Regent V models for East Kent, seen in the bodybuilder's works yard, just before delivery in February 1966 — note the Sheffield Leyland Atlantean reflected in the side panels. Theses vehicles had AV590 engines as indicated by the 2D3RA chassis number prefix, this being 2D3RA1825, but East Kent's final batch delivered the following year, and the last Regents for an English operator, were 3D3RA models with the 11.3-litre AV690 unit. The prominent AEC letters on the grille had been introduced to suit the more exhibitionist mood of the times.

Generally accepted as the last Regent, Douglas Corporation's No. 15 (410 LMN) had the final D-series chassis number, 3D2RA2024 and entered service in December 1968. Willowbrook built the 65-seat forward-entrance bodywork.

The last variants of the Regent V to be introduced were the 3D-series models with AV690 engine, of which Southampton Corporation was the first and largest user. Number 392 (JCR 392E), on chassis 3D2RA1871, seen during a road test carried out by the author for Bus & Coach, was the last of twelve delivered in January-February 1967 which had bodywork built at Blackburn by East Lancashire — an initial batch of eight dating from 1966 and the final ten delivered later in 1967 had almost identical bodywork built at the Neepsend premises in Sheffield. Despite the large-capacity engine, performance fully laden was not as lively as had been possible 20 years earlier with early Regent III buses.

Pontypridd Urban District Council could claim the distinction of being the last to place AEC Regent buses in service, as two of its 2MD3RA buses did not enter service until March 1969. Number 6 (NNY 763E), seen here after the 1974 change of name to Taff Ely District Council, was a slightly earlier vehicle, with the preceding chassis number 2MD3RA642 (numerically the fourth last MD-series Regent), and the last of seven with Metro-Cammell bodywork placed in service in July 1967.

Ipswich (four 2D2RA), St. Helens (three 2D3RA) and Felix Motors, an independent based at Hatfield, near Doncaster, which had regularly taken single examples.

West Pakistan took 50 3D2RA in 1967, followed by Rotherham Corporation, an operator not previously a Regent user (though five Bridgemasters were in the fleet) with an order for three and East Kent's final batch consisted of fifteen of the synchromesh version, numbered 3D3RA2007-2021, registered MFN 938-952F. The last of these to enter service, MFN 946F, took to the road in January 1968 and was the last Regent V for an English operator. The chassis number 2022 in this series, like quite a number of other late ones, was not used, doubtless due to a cancelled order.

The numerical last MD-series chassis, 2MD3RA645, entered service as MSN 863G with the Garelochhead fleet later in 1968, but the last two 'heavy' Regents were Douglas Corporation's 3D2RA2023-24, numbered 14 and 15 (409 and 410 LMN) which took the road in December of that year. However, the last two vehicles to enter service were Pontypridd's last two 2MD3RA, numbered just before the Garelochhead example at 2MD3RA643-4, and registered UTG 312-3G, which entered service in March 1969. Like the Douglas vehicles they had Willowbrook forward-entrance bodywork.

The first operator to see the possibilities of building double-deck bodywork on a slightly modified version of the left-hand-drive Regal III chassis was the Barcelona Tramways undertaking, which had previously operated double-decker motor buses dating from the 'twenties. An initial batch of 25 chassis, officially ACLO Regent III models, was built in the June-September 1947 period and one of these, which were numbered O963577-601, was selected as the basis of the prototype vehicle numbered 401 seen here during a demonstration run immediately after completion in February 1948. The choice of centre-entrance layout may well have been inspired by the West Riding concern's use of this layout for the bodywork on the first batch of right-hand Regent III models, as shown on page 18, though the other aspects of design are quite different and the 17ft. 6in. wheelbase allowed a higher seating capacity of 59, with 33 on top — the photograph indicates that the staircase was immediately behind the entrance. Escoriaza built the body on this and 44 further buses of similar style but slightly different layout mostly delivered in 1949. The rear-entrance bodies by Macosa built on 25 more Regent III buses, five in 1948 and the rest in 1953, were reputedly to a much older style derived from a 1927 pattern.

Chapter ten:
The left-handers

Reference had been made in previous chapters to exports of right-hand-drive models and the special versions built to suit overseas markets. The story of the left-hand-drive Regents has been given a chapter of its own, partly because it amounted to far more than a version of the standard chassis with left-hand steering and partly because the various models were given chassis numbers in different series and thus form a family of their own.

It had been standard practice to offer the forward-control AEC models only with right-hand steering until 1946. Even for countries where traffic drove on the right, this was often regarded as quite acceptable — in Europe there were several countries where right-hand steering was usual for the heavier types of commercial vehicle. However, AEC was keen to exploit export opportunities in South America where right-hand-drive Regal single-deckers had been sold in encouraging numbers

but where United States influence meant that left-hand steering was much preferred.

It was decided to build a true left-hand Regal Mark III chassis, almost a mirror image of the right-hand version, in which not only the steering but the construction of the 9.6-litre engine, type A207 in this form, and the whole layout of the chassis were changed over. Like many AEC chassis, this had angled engine and transmission centre lines and these were all faithfully switched over from the home-market version. The interest foreseen was concentrated on single-deckers and the O963 model was

originally offered only as such. By early 1947 hundreds of them were being built, largely for Argentina, Brazil and Uruguay but also for several European countries.

The shorter of the two standard export Regal III wheelbase lengths was 17ft. 6in. and thus it was not difficult to construct a double-deck version directly equivalent to the export Regent III right-hand model of the same dimensions. This possibility seems to have been picked up almost immediately in Barcelona and the first such chassis were being built in June 1947. For some reason, no announcement was made at the time,

The mirror-image effect, with the whole transmission line switched over to the opposite side as well as a true 'left-handed' engine and opposite-hand driver's controls, is conveyed by comparing this drawing of an early Regal III O963 left-hand chassis with those on pages 17 and 41. Under AEC's drawing office system, the prefix Z was used for chassis miscellaneous items and thus chassis arrangement drawings were given the model number with Z prefix, hence ZO963 in this case.

The extent to which AEC went to produce a genuine left-handed engine for the left-hand drive chassis is shown in these two views. Above is seen a normal home-market A218 engine as seen, in this case, in one of the Regent V D3RV chassis with Regent III-style front-end built for Nottingham in 1966 – No. 266 (XTO 266) on D3RV243, now preserved. Below is seen Leyland Vehicles' own ex-Lisbon Regal III, recently donated by the operator and on permanent loan to the Friends of the British Commercial Vehicle Museum, showing the engine to A217 specification (in both cases the water pipe running over the exhaust manifold was the key feature signifying the change from the early post-war A208 and A207 versions respectively, though early units were often modified). Access to the servicing points visible plus others reached by removing the bonnet side panel was thus equally good on the left-hand model, certainly not true of other British makers' attempts at left-hand forward-control front-engined bus chassis.

but the June 1948 issue of 'AEC Gazette', the company's house journal, reported that an order had been placed for 100 ACLO Regent Mark III double-deckers, to be operated in Barcelona by Sociedad Financiera Industrias y Transportes S.A, and that bodies were being supplied by Maquinaria y Elementos de Transporte. A photograph, reproduced herewith, shows a vehicle with centre-entrance body, described as the first example on test. 'ACLO' was the sales name adopted for AEC in Spanish-speaking countries when the German AEG concern objected to the normal initials.

It seems that the order was later reduced to 50, the chassis numbers O963577-626 appearing in AEC's records as having been built for completion as double-deckers, chassis construction having been completed by June 1948. Of these, 45 had 59-seat centre-entrance bodywork actually built by Escoriaza and the remaining five had 61-seat rear-entrance bodies by Macosa, all entering service in 1948-49. However, 20 more with similar Macosa bodies were built in 1953, and of these fifteen of the chassis, 9631E633-647, had numbers apparently allocated from the original order, the remainder being 9631E1420-24.

The next, and in the long run very important, customer for left-hand-drive Regents was Lisbon Electric Tramways Ltd, then a London-based company although also known by its Portuguese title, Companhia Carris de Ferro di Lisboa. It had first purchased AEC Regent buses in 1940, but these were neither double-deck nor left-hand. The double-deck type chassis — basically standard contemporary O661/19 models with 7.7-litre engines — had Weymann single-deck bodywork with only 28 seats but designed to carry a big standee load in connection with the centenary exhibition of that year. Major expansion of bus services came after the war and the company, in those days British-owned, returned to AEC for most of its needs. Some 91 of the O963 or, from 1948, 9631E chassis were fitted with single-deck bodies, entering service between 1948 and 1950, and it is noteworthy that these too are sometimes quoted as Regent rather than Regal.

The first Lisbon AEC double-deckers were built in 1950, having chassis numbers originally allocated to Barcelona, 9631E627-632, though it is not clear whether the chassis had been built as such or the numbers merely

reallocated. They received Weymann 58-seat bodywork of a style related to the contemporary home-market product and virtually a mirror image of a design built by MCW's South African associate. Thenceforth double-deckers of this type were to be standard until 1956. A batch of 25 entered service in 1951-52 and was followed by the rebodying in 1953-54 of four of the single-deckers of the pre-1950 period, plus 27 on new chassis and 22 more were added in 1955-56.

Meanwhile, another user had appeared. Baghdad Passenger Transport Service had been set up following a study of that city's needs by consultants from London Transport. Here too the initial choice had been of AEC Regal III left-hand-drive single-deckers, though in this case the crash-gearbox vacuum-brake version, type 9631A. This was a model virtually exclusive to Baghdad, though five chassis were supplied to AEC's agents in Portugal and one to an operator with an address in Kingston, Jamaica, a few months before the initial batch of 100 were ready for shipment to Baghdad in June 1951, complete with Park Royal bodywork. It used the same venerable D124 gearbox as the home-market 9612A etc but with a rather

It is an almost uncanny experience — like penetrating the world on the opposite side of a mirror — to watch the driver at work in one of the ex-Lisbon vehicles now preserved in this country. The hands reach for the familiar-looking controls, but it is the preselector control that is on the right and the handbrake on the left, rather than vice-versa. The preselector lever works in exactly the same fashion as on the right-hand model but is built up from opposite-hand castings.

Lisbon Electric Tramways Ltd, in later years better known by the Portuguese name, Carris (literally ''rail'') or the initials CCFL, took 91 of the O963 or 9631E chassis, quoted in the operator's records as Regent III, though supplied with single-deck bodywork by Weymann or Saunders.

Double-deck bodywork began to be supplied in 1950 and batches to this general design with Weymann 58-seat bodywork and based on Regent III 9631E chassis followed annually until 1956, some of the vehicles being stored at the AEC works after bodying while awaiting shipment. The front bumper had yet to be added and the radiator was covered by protective coating.

Baghdad Passenger Transport Service took delivery of two batches of 100 Regal III single-deckers, choosing the 9631A model, with crash gearbox, and then, in 1953 and following on from the second of these, 20 double-deckers, all these vehicles being bodied by Park Royal. The general appearance was not dissimilar to the Lisbon design, although based on Park Royal's standard design of the period. They looked quite striking in bright red and cream, with silver roof. The triangular emblem on the side was clearly derived from AEC's badge outline and included a reproduction of the AEC radiator outline between the wings.

awkward-looking linkage to match what was in essence a right-hand gearbox to a left-hand model.

After Baghdad's second batch of 100 single-deckers came a further 20 with suspension, etc to suit double-deck bodywork and these, 9631A1660-1679, were also bodied by Park Royal being completed by February and June 1953. So far as is known, a total of 170 of the 963-series chassis received double-deck bodywork from new. It was thus very much a minority choice, representing less than 9 per cent of the total, but even so, AEC had already built far more left-hand-drive double-deckers than any other British manufacturer. This was quite an achievement for a model which seems to have been something of an afterthought. There had been a curious announcement in 'AEC Gazette' for February 1949 to the effect that the model number 9661E "should be added" to the list of production models representing the left-hand-drive 8ft.-wide Regent Mark III with 17ft. 6in. wheelbase. Yet 9631E had continued to be used for such vehicles.

The left-hand Regent V

The prospects for left-hand double-decker sales were seen more clearly when the Mark V range was introduced. A D2LA model was listed almost immediately, with the usual 17ft. 6in. overseas wheelbase, the general left-hand characteristics including the 9.6-litre engine, which had graduated to type A217 at the same time as the home-market units had switched to A218, and at first retaining the traditional radiator. The 4in.-wide springs were, as with the right-hand models, the key characteristic but the standard chassis had the Monocontrol transmission. An 11.3-litre A222 engine, again left-hand, was a listed option.

The first customer was Lisbon Electric Tramways, becoming increasingly known by the CCFL initials, and D2LA001-028, delivered in 1957, were noteworthy in having preselective gearboxes and thus were almost identical in specification to the previous Regent III buses in this fleet, with only the Mark V frame and springs as distinguishing features. With traditional-style Weymann rear-entrance bodywork, they represented a closer continuation of the original Mark III concept than any home-market Regent V variant.

The next customer was the Teheran Omnibus Board in Iran, from whom a remarkable first order for 250 D2LA models was secured, D2LA029-278. These, too, were 17ft. 6in. wheelbase chassis but had A222 11.3-litre engines, Monocontrol transmission and a left-hand version of the standard Regent V new-look front-end, though the addition of a front bumper modified the appearance. Park Royal got the body contract, building a 73-seat design derived from its contemporary

This line-up of Lisbon Regent III and, in the centre and left of the picture, Regent V buses, all with Weymann bodywork, was evidently taken soon after the arrival of the 1959 delivery. The vehicle nearest the camera on the right is No. 263 (DA-21-92) on chassis 9613E1701 dating from 1954.

Teheran, like Baghdad, sought London Transport expertise in the development of its transport system. The result was the adoption of vehicles having much in common in make, type, bodywork and even livery. Teheran's first order broke new ground in being the first left-hand Regent models to have the new-look front end virtually as used for the home-market Regent V which by then had succeeded the Regent III. The first left-hand Regent V models, for

Lisbon, had the earlier model's external appearance as well as preselective gearboxes, but Teheran were basically standard D2LA with Monocontrol semi-automatic transmission. One of the first of the 250 vehicles on chassis D2LA029-278 is seen after completion and (right) undergoing tilt test at London Transport's Chiswick works, the latter picture dated 13th March 1958.

home-market standard. Delivered in 1958, this single order outnumbered all other AEC double-decker deliveries put together that year, turning what would have been a poor year into one of the best for the Regent V model.

Lisbon took another 38 chassis in the 1958-59 period, this time of a newly-introduced LD2LA type, with 18ft. 7in. wheelbase — like the home-market version with L prefix. The remainder of the specification was generally similar to the Teheran chassis but they had Weymann bodywork of a 67-seat forward-entrance layout. By contrast, the first and a subsequent Baghdad Regent V batch had the home-market 16ft. 4in. wheelbase length, but the chassis specification was otherwise similar to the other contemporary D2LA standard—Baghdad now accepting

the Monocontrol transmission. Park Royal again got the body contract, the rear-entrance bodies seating 65. The first 100, D2LA317-416, were built in 1958-59 and 80 more, D2LA505-584, followed in 1961.

From 1959 until the end of left-hand Regent V production in 1967, orders came almost entirely from the same group of sources — Baghdad, Teherhan and Portugal or Portuguese overseas territories. Thus three buses to contemporary CCFL Lisbon pattern complete with similar Weymann bodywork, went to Luanda in Angola in 1959, followed by five more in 1960-61. Orders for operation in Lisbon continued to have the LD2LA chassis designation to the end of production for this operator in 1965, unlike home-market 18ft. 7in. wheelbase chassis where the L prefix had been phased

out by 1959. This did not apply to other 18ft. 7in. left-hand models, even when intended for other Portuguese operators and having similar bodywork to the Lisbon buses, which were simply D2LA, suggesting that the prefix letter was being used latterly to signify 'Lisbon'.

The long-standing association of Weymann and the Lisbon fleet began to be broken in 1960, when two vehicles out of a batch of 20 were bodied by the UTIC concern, set up by Portuguese operators as a co-operative venture. The company operating local services in Oporto, STCP, took delivery of ten similar buses and subsequent orders for Lisbon were bodied either by UTIC or by the CCFL workshops themselves — a further 20 in 1960-61, 30 in 1961-62, 48 in 1962-63 and nine in 1964. A few months before the

The vehicles for the next Baghdad order, on chassis D2LA317-416, were similar in general specification and appearance to the 1958 Teheran buses but were on slightly shorter 16ft. 4in. wheelbase chassis and most were supplied with bodywork in this 'partly knocked down' form, with the lower deck completed as a shell in which were housed parts to allow completion on arrival. This reduced shipping costs and provided employment at the destination — factors growing in importance. They were shipped in 1958-59.

Through the mid-to-late 'fifties and much of the 'sixties, export orders for Regents and especially left-hand-drive models for the Middle-East played a major part in keeping both the AEC and Park Royal factories busy. This view shows the scene in Park Royal's works in the spring of 1966 as the last Regent contract for 100 buses for Baghdad went through. These were again based on 16ft. 4in.-wheelbase D2LA chassis and the vehicle in the foreground is believed to be D2LA1022, shipped in May of that year. These retained the rear-entrance layout as on previous contracts. A noteworthy detail of the D2LA model is the detachable panel above the main radiator grille opening (and behind the bodybuilder's identification tag bearing the body number B54687 in this view). This allowed the A217 or A222 engine, taller than the AV590 used on home-market models, to be withdrawn through the front panel once the bumper and lower panel had been removed.

last-mentioned batch, one 18ft. 7in.-wheelbase chassis, D2LA633, was exported in April 1963 to the Pando company (fleet name COPSA) in Montevideo, Uruguay, being thought to be the only post-war Regent to go to South America. Two vehicles with UTIC bodies went to Coimbra Municipality in Portugal, one of which was evidently diverted from the last-mentioned Lisbon order which called for ten chassis. Five more buses went to Luanda, also in 1963.

The next order for the Lisbon fleet comprised 31 sets of chassis units, given the numbers LD2LA650-680 and delivered in 1964, used in the construction of integral double-deckers by UTIC. This development may have been inspired by London Transport's Routemaster fleet, for which AEC had been building sets of units in numbers comparable to the total Regent output from 1959, though UTIC clearly favoured a more orthodox basic design. A further 30 complete Regent chassis for Lisbon followed in 1965-66, plus one supplied via UTIC to another operator, but 26 more sets of units, LD2LA776-801, were supplied to UTIC in 1965 for further vehicles for Lisbon, those numbers following 64 left unused, apparently due to a cancelled order.

Finally both Teheran, with 200 chassis numbered D2LA802-1001 and Baghdad, with 100 taking the chassis numbers up to D2LA1101, again dominated the output of Regents in 1966-67. All had Park Royal bodywork, but only one of the Teheran buses was completed in Britain, the rest being sent out in sets of parts. They were on 18ft. 7in. wheelbase chassis with two-door bodywork, though the main entrance and stairs were at the front. The last chassis numbers were allocated to 28 chassis sent to Baghdad for use as spares, D2LA1102-1129, eight of them without engines.

The left-hand Regent V had retained the traditional type of engine as originally developed in the Mark III era, latterly in A222 11.3-litre form. This was done because the AV-series engines were not available in left-hand form. However, the apparent 'holding back' to an obsolete unit was probably a kindness, as it seems likely that the cooling system and related gasket problems experienced by some, though not all, users of these engines in Britain would have been aggravated in the hotter climate of Portugal and, especially, the Middle East. When rear-engined buses succeeded the Regents — Daimler Fleetlines in Portugal and Leyland Atlanteans in Baghdad and Teheran — overheating required modifications, whereas the Regents were to prove very reliable.

79352

The final Teheran batch of 200 Regent models built in 1966-67 were on 18ft. 7in. wheelbase chassis and had two-doorway 71-seat bodywork though the staircase and main entrance door was at the front. The Park Royal body design was derived from the contemporary home-market standard design, and although this retained the high upper-deck waist level, the livery style and such details as the polished full-depth sliding window frames gave a purposeful and less austere overall effect than usual. The batch were on chassis D2LA802-1001.

Although looking just like a typical left-hand Regent V with Weymann bodywork, this vehicle is in fact one of the U.T.I.C. integral double-deckers built for the Lisbon CCFL fleet in 1964-66, officially described as UTIC-AEC Regent V. There were 57 and although having UTIC serial numbers, they were based on sets of AEC units which were given numbers in the left-hand Regent V series, as described in the text. The vehicle shown is No. 690, registered GE-92-80, which is U2007-046 in the UTIC series, which ran from U2007-001 to U2007-057. As well as the conformity to standard Regent V practice in all visible parts of the 'chassis', the bodywork has strong Weymann characteristics in the general outline, apart from a somewhat squared-up rear-end, as well as such items as the outswept skirt and cab window outlines. It is seen in service in 1978.

Night-time pictures often tend to be rich in atmosphere and this scene in Nottingham, captured by the camera of the unrivalled Geoff Atkins in a crisp night in January 1950 is a case in point. Three Regents in the fleet of Midland General Omnibus Co Ltd, all with Weymann bodywork, await departure time. Nearest the camera is No. 117 (MRB 40), one of fifteen Regent III models placed in service a little over a year earlier, this one being 9612E3736. Behind is No. 125 (KRB 75), a Regent II, O6618018, dating from 1947, and third in line a pre-war forward-entrance example. Despite the obvious family affinities of outline between the first two, there would have been a marked difference in sound effects as they moved off. The Regent III's preselective gearbox

would have emitted the usual muffled clonk as the air-pressure closed the epicyclic band to engage gear and then, with a soft exhaust burble and the rather melodious whine of this type of gearbox, it would be away, the 9.6-litre engine accelerating without fuss. The Regent II's 7.7-litre engine would not have sounded all that different at tick-over but the almost vintage-style and unmistakably 'AEC' crash gearbox note, more strident than the preselector, even if nowadays music to the nostalgic ear, would have been evident as soon as it moved off. The smaller engine would have probably sounded as if working a little harder, though actual exhaust noise was quite 'soft' in both cases.

Chapter eleven:
Post-war Regents in retrospect

Interchangeability of many Regent II components with those of pre-war models often led to such exchanges taking place and here Liverpool Corporation's HKA 383 on chassis O6617968, which entered service in August 1947, carries a pre-1938 radiator when seen at Penny Lane just after being renumbered from A299 to A499 nearly a decade later. This view also shows Liverpool's variation on cab front design in the Weymann-framed body as finished by Edge Lane works.

The Regent II was more obviously 'on the way out' even when first introduced than any of its direct contemporaries. AEC's highly effective publicity had built up interest in the Regent III in a way which made the Mark II model an obvious stop-gap. Yet it had quite a lot going for it — reliable, efficient and, though perhaps a trivial-seeming

factor, free from the taint of wartime austerity and thus visually acceptable at a time when people wanted to leave the wartime gloom behind.

Judged in a more practical light, it could be relied upon to give trouble-free service over long periods. Occasionally, at extended mileages, the 7.7-litre engine's timing could slip, resulting in an odd-sounding rumbly engine note but this was easily rectified and no harm would generally have occurred. By the late 'fifties, BET companies tended to be working on about a twelve-year vehicle life policy, so vehicles purchased in 1946-48 were being withdrawn around 1958-60 but many of them, especially those with Weymann metal-framed bodywork, saw further service with independent operators or contractors. Wider variation was to be found elsewhere, the Mansfield District and Midland

London Transport's solitary batch of post-war STL-class buses, the 20 Regent II models with standard 'provincial' Weymann bodywork, were significantly modernised in appearance by the application of the almost all-green livery. Seen here at Watford is STL2691 (HGC 224), on O6617500 which had entered service in February 1946 — it was one of those which later passed to the Dundee fleet as described below.

(Below) Although still in good condition, the post-war STL buses were all sold in 1955 when London Transport found itself with a surplus of buses. All 20 found good homes with municipal fleets, but the most interesting from a mechanical viewpoint were the ten purchased by Dundee Corporation, which promptly fitted preselective gearboxes, producing a combination of 7.7-litre A173 engine and this form of transmission common in the late 'thirties but not offered by AEC in the post-war era. Dundee's No. 172 (HGC 220), on chassis O6617496, is seen below between pre-war and wartime Daimlers — it had started life as STL2687.

(Below right) Grimsby Corporation took six of the post-war STL buses, including HGC 227, which was O6617504 and had been STL2694, remaining in service with what by then was Grimsby-Cleethorpes as No. 44 until January 1967, by which date it was 21 years old.

Believed to have been the earliest Regent II buses to be sold off were six of Leicester Corporation's immediate post-war batch, exchanged for four Devon General Regal single-deckers of almost similar age in 1952. Significantly, the vehicles chosen all had the Park Royal 'relaxed utility' bodies, leaving only one of this type alongside the seven Weymann-bodied examples, all of which were retained. Here DJF 326 on chassis O6617513 is seen in Devon General livery, having become DR700 in the latter's fleet.

Body condition was apt to be a problem on vehicles with wood-framed body structure built in the period when good-quality seasoned timber was virtually unobtainable. Newcastle Corporation's No. 37 (JVK 637) on chassis O6613462 had been one of the last of that city's delivery of Regent II models, entering service in March 1946, and one of the seven with Park Royal bodywork. It is seen here as running in the 'fifties, with rounded ends to the lower deck windows added more as a means of disguising the bracing of the framing that had been applied rather than any intention of toning down the 'utility' appearance.

A more radical course had been taken by the independent operator T. Burrows & Sons of Wombwell, near Barnsley, in Yorkshire. Number 55 (FWX 869) on chassis O6617839, dating from 1947, had been one of four Regent II models in this fleet, all of which originally had Strachans lowbridge bodywork to what was virtually relaxed utility specification. It is seen here after receiving a new Roe highbridge body in July 1956, a style familiar on the Regent III but not on this earlier chassis type — in fact Roe had not built any bodies on the Regent II chassis. Rebodying of the Regent II was a very rare occurrence, however.

General examples running for a minimum of fifteen and in several cases over eighteen years, and while Leicester's 1946 fleet was withdrawn in 1959 (apart from some examples exchanged with Devon General in 1952 for AEC Regal single-deckers), Reading still had all of its 1948 batch in service in 1963.

A noteworthy example of further service was London Transport's final 20 vehicles in the STL class, new in

1946. Sold in 1955 as LT found itself with a surplus of vehicles, all re-entered service in municipal fleets, ten with Dundee, six with Grimsby and four with Widnes. The Dundee buses were the most interesting case as they were converted from crash gearbox to preselective, an alteration that would have been a logical move for LT to make had its fleet needs been greater, and remained in operation in this form until the end of 1964. Most of

Grimsby's examples lasted until 1967 and one, the former STL2692, until January 1968, when it was one of the last of the type still in use with a major operator, happily surviving for restoration to original condition.

As explained in earlier chapters, the Regent III had benefitted from the wartime service experience with the so-called 'pre-war' RT fleet in London. A few potential teething troubles did remain to emerge in varying operating

London Transport's vehicle surplus also led to the premature sale of the Cravens-bodied RT-type buses. At a time when any post-war double-deckers were still a rarity on the second-hand vehicle market, they were soon snapped up. Here JXC 181, chassis number O9611375, the former RT1422 and one of the first of the type, dating from March 1949, is seen in the depot of Lowland Motorways Ltd in Shettleston, Glasgow, in July 1956 soon after purchase and repainting in that concern's livery, having become number 38. In January 1958 the Lowland business passed to Scottish Omnibuses Ltd and Lowland's fleet of six ex-London Cravens RT-type buses were among the vehicles taken into the SOL fleet, this one taking the fleet number B31 by then vacated by a wartime 'unfrozen' Regent, remaining in service until 1963.

To some fleets, the Regent III was close to the ideal. Bradford Corporation, faced with a need for major bus fleet expansion as the result of tramway replacement in 1949-50, placed in service a batch of 40 examples of the 9612E model in 8ft.-wide form, with the 'classic' style of Weymann bodywork in its most handsome form. Chassis number 9612E4353, No. 7 (FKY 7) is seen in the AEC works drive at Southall before delivery in November 1949,

the works photographer producing this sparkling portrait. Bradford's post-war light blue and cream livery with dark grey roof suited these buses particularly well. Though other makes were purchased to augment the fleet, the Regent in various subsequent forms was to remain standard until the 'sixties.

In others, much the same type of bus was very much an odd-man-out. When the Red & White group was in control of a string of operators in southern England as well as Wales, the preselective Regent III had been chosen as the immediate post-war standard for the former, all of which had a proportion of routes of urban or partly urban character. However, when these fleets came into Tilling group control after Red & White sold out in 1950, they became completely non-standard. This particular bus, chassis number O9611881, had rather a complex life, being one of seven with Weymann-design bodywork assembled by R & W's bodybuilding offshoot, Lydney Coachworks, early in 1948 and originally intended for the Venture Ltd fleet at Basingstoke but this one was diverted firstly to Cheltenham & District, where it was registered HAD 745, and then to Newbury & District in 1949 before becoming No. 99 at Venture after all in January 1950, just before Venture came under the wing of Wilts & Dorset as a result of the Tilling-group takeover. Fortunately, W & D seemed to treat these vehicles with respect, not altering their specification, and the concern's Salisbury paint shop turned them out in smart condition as conveyed by this picture of what by then was No. 499 taken at the former Venture garage in Victoria Street, Basingstoke. It remained in service until 1962.

A very different interpretation of the Regent III/Weymann combination emerged from Liverpool Corporation's specification, which took most of the subtle curvature out of the characteristic profile. This unusual pure side view shows A671 (JKF 914) on chassis 9612E4403 as it emerges from Edge Lane works after the Weymann-built shell had been completed and finished there in March 1950. This was one of 100 preselective-transmission Regents of similar type placed in service between December 1949 and August 1951, mostly completed by Edge Lane, although a minority were farmed out to local bodybuilding concerns.

conditions, such as a little bit too much of the engine mounting flexibility which gave the model much of its refinement, leading to instances of the engine touching the side panel of the cab on some early provincial examples, as well as the instances of overheating which led to the slightly modified A218 engine. Generally, reliability was good and the accessibility of items for servicing popular with garage staff.

Drivers almost always liked the model, especially in preselective form, and AEC's publicity image of it as a superior sort of bus was in many ways justified. A few operators clearly felt that elaboration had gone too far and, in an extreme example, after the three examples dating from 1947-48 in the Cheltenham District Traction Co fleet came under the Bristol Tramways & Carriage Co Ltd's umbrella, they were converted to 7.7-litre engine, crash gearbox and vacuum brakes in 1953-54.

Potentially, as was to become evident, the model, in either RT or provincial form, had immense capability for long life. Oddly enough, London Transport, ultimately to prove the point, was the first major operator to sell post-war RT-type buses due to

the surplus that had arisen as operating needs fell short of expectations. Both the Cravens-bodied batch (of which 30 went to Dundee, obviously impressed with ex-London buses) and some early standard examples were sold as early as 1956-57. However, London subsequently tended to slow down the disposal of AEC RT-type buses until the Leyland RTL and RTW types had been sold off.

As a result, the number of RT-type buses licensed for passenger service with London Transport remained almost static at about 3,700 from 1964 until 1968, and there were still over 1,000 in service up to the end of 1973 — some 484 had left the fleet at one go as the result of the hiving off of the country area to the newly-formed London Country Bus Services Ltd on 1st January 1970. London Country was keen to replace these latter by vehicles suitable for one-man operation — a process causing the demise of numerous rear-entrance double-deckers including many Regent models in a wide variety of fleets — but, in the event, RT reliability as contrasted to the troubles experienced with much more modern rear-engined buses kept an admittedly

dwindling number in London Country service until 1978. London Transport itself still had twelve examples in public service up to 7th April, 1979, when the final journey was operated by RT624, then in theory over 30 years old, though LTE overhaul policy meant that it would be fairer to put an average age of about 27-28 years on these last surviving chassis, due to interchange of units and, indeed, complete chassis despite the dubious legality of the latter.

In the provinces, the life of Regent III models varied considerably. In general, BET companies followed their twelve-year life policy, give or take a year or two, whereas most municipalities and some of the other companies kept such vehicles for longer, sometimes considerably so. Thus, Rhondda's RT-type Regents, and even some of its earlier provincial-type Regent III buses dating from 1946-48 were withdrawn in 1958, whereas Aberdeen's almost identical buses of 1946-47 ran until 1966-67. In some cases, as with some Regent II models, body condition was the determining factor — timber quality on composite bodies built in the early post-war years was apt to be poor.

The long life achieved by some of the RT buses was partly due to London Transport's high standards of overhaul. Here RT520 (HLX 337), a 'top-box' example originally placed in service in March 1948, looks like a new bus after emerging from Aldenham works in the 'fifties. Full destination blinds had been fitted and the livery altered to the style having only one cream band — the latter was widely agreed to be a retrograde step adopted as an economy.

The body originally built by Chiswick works in 1939 for RT1 took on a new lease of life after RT19, which had been fitted with it in 1945 (as shown on page 17), was withdrawn with all the other surviving 'pre-war' RT buses in 1955. It re-emerged in June 1956 mounted on the chassis from one of the Cravens-bodied batch of RT buses, RT1420 dating from March 1949, to act as a mobile instruction unit with similar duties to the former Tilling ST-bodied unit shown on page 21. It was given the service vehicle fleet number 1037J and operated on trade plates as shown in this picture taken in the late 'sixties. When pensioned off in 1978, it was purchased by the late Prince Marshall and restored as 'RT1'.

Sold-off RT-type buses took on some unfamiliar liveries but none stranger than Hull Corporation's 'streamline' blue and cream. The vehicles in question were in fact from the St. Helens Corporation fleet, No. 35 (BDJ 818) on chassis O9617143, seen here being one of nine of the batch built in 1952 purchased by Hull together with ten of the 1950 batch in 1962. Curiously, the London destination display accepted by St. Helens was rejected at Hull and that undertaking's standard substituted.

Rebodying of AEC Regent III models was rare, most of the original bodies being of durable construction. This vehicle, on chassis 9612E3716 registered JVO 942 and originally No. 146 in the Mansfield District fleet when placed in service in 1948, was one of twelve transferred to the associated Notts & Derby fleet when that concern ceased trolleybus operation in 1953 but suffered accident damage sufficient to justify replacement of the original Weymann body by the new Eastern Coach Works highbridge 58-seat body shown in 1955. The result is believed to be a unique combination of Regent III chassis with ECW body — oddly enough ECW used a five-bay design rather than the contemporary four-bay style used mainly on Bristol KS-series chassis which it otherwise somewhat resembles. It is seen at Mount Street, Nottingham, soon after re-entering service.

Operators' policy with vehicles taken over with acquired businesses varied. Potteries Motor Traction Co Ltd took over the independent Tilstone concern of Tunstall in June 1951, running it as a subsidiary at first before absorbing it completely the following February. With an already mixed fleet, PMT kept this preselective Regent III, chassis number O9612616, placed in service by Tilstone in 1949. It was rather an unusual vehicle being lowbridge and 8ft. wide with bodywork by Strachans. It is seen here in Longton in 1958 as PMT L416, looking a little past its best, though possibly the most curious feature was the high cab waist level, an idea not uncommon in much earlier times but rarely so pronounced as in this case. It survived until 1963.

By contrast, this Nottingham City Transport Regent III, No. 1097 (KTV 107) on chassis 9612E4208 is seen within a month or so of entering service. It was one of 30 with Metro-Cammell bodywork built to that bodybuilder's standard outline for this chassis, derived from an old design by the bodybuilder and 'frozen' for the provincial Regent III by being selected for an order built for Salford in 1947. It seemed dated at the time but in retrospect can be seen as well-proportioned and in many ways more attractive than much of what was to follow in the 'fifties. The flat front hub cap, with coloured AEC emblem, was introduced in place of the earlier domed type used since 1931 at just about the same time as the switch from O961 to 9612E or 9612A prefix chassis numbers, on chassis constructed from about the beginning of 1948 onwards.

The rivals. AEC's Regent III and Leyland's Titan PD2 family (including London variants) were running almost neck and neck in terms of production figures with AEC marginally in front at the end of RT production in 1954, but Leyland drew ahead in later years. Here the West Monmouthshire Omnibus Board's No. 28 (HWO 189) on Regent III chassis 9612E2641, one of a pair with Bruce lowbridge bodywork dating from 1949 is seen alongside No. 21 (260 BAX), a Leyland PD2/40 with Massey body also of the lowbridge type dating from 1961.

In others, cracking of chassis frames attributable to the AEC stabiliser was sufficient to kill off some otherwise fit if elderly buses. Even so, many more examples of the type might well have survived into the 'seventies had the rear-entrance double-decker not gone out of favour from an operational viewpoint. When the original four Passenger Transport Executives came into operation in the October 1969-January 1970 period, only Liverpool Corporation handed over any substantial number of Regent III models, just over half the 100 final full-width bonnet batch surviving into the Merseyside PTE era.

The Regent V story was often one of life curtailment by events to an even greater extent, as one-man operation was a widespread objective by the time the earlier ones were due for withdrawal, even on a twelve-year life scale. In any case the AV470-powered mediumweight versions were hardly long-life designs, at least if used on intensive service, especially when

fitted with the more austere types of lightweight bodywork, though Aberdeen extended the life of some by fitting Gardner 6LW engines. The A218-engined and related overseas versions were directly comparable to the Mark III they so closely resembled and if the later AV590 was not to prove quite so rugged an engine in some fleets it gave good service in others (a comment also applicable to the AV470). However, it is fair to say that the Regent V did not have the enthusiasm-fostering backing of AEC's management and even the publicity department in the way that had applied to the Mark III. The division of emphasis among three families of double-decker left the Regent V as the poor relation as compared to the Bridgemaster, Routemaster and Renown models of more modern design, though it was to outnumber them all.

Even so, the 'final scores' underlined that the real success story in terms of sales was centred on the Regent III in

9.6-litre form, and 58 per cent of the right-hand examples of these were RT-type buses for London. The following are the total numbers of vehicles built, as classified by the chassis number series. Numbers not used due to cancelled orders account for the totals being less, in most cases, than those of the highest chassis numbers issued.

In 1964, there were over 8,000 AEC Regent buses in service with major operators in Britain, a total second only to the 10,000-odd Leyland Titans among individual double-decker models. Nearly half the Regent total were London RT-type buses and this ratio remained almost unchanged by the end of 1970 when the Regent total had fallen to just over 5,000.

During the 'seventies, the rate of withdrawals increased and by 1978 the figure was not much over 500 and by 1980 barely 120, of which almost half, 58, were with one operator, the East Kent Road Car Co, with Southampton in second place with eighteen. By this point, several of the surviving vehicles

Model	Chassis number range	Totals built	
Regent II (7.7)	O6617401 — O6618095	695	695
Regent III (9.6)	O961001 — 9613E8261 etc	8325*	
Regent III (7.7)	6811A001 — 6812A136	138§	8633
Regent III (L.H.)	(Various between O963577 and 9631E1853)	170**	
Regent V (AV470)	MD3RV001 — 2MD3RA645	641	
Regent V (9.6 etc)	D3RV001 — 3D2RA2024	1961	3702
Regent V (6LW)	D2RV6G001 — D2RA6G120	120	
Regent V (L.H.)	D2LA001 — D2LA1129	980§§	
			Total 13030

* Excludes 46 export-type 9612E chassis built for Sydney but converted to Regal III in 1949-50 and renumbered in 9621E series before sale to British operators, and includes 125 fire-engine chassis, given Maudslay chassis numbers D62001R — D62115R and D63001R — D63010R, although five of the latter were originally built as M9613A10001 — 10005. These were of standard 16ft. 4in. wheelbase, whereas the D62001R series were 13ft. 6in.
§ Includes two prototype chassis numbered in U series.
** Total comprises those chassis known to have been built for or completed as double-deckers.
§§ Excludes 57 sets of units supplied to UTIC for integral vehicles and 28 chassis built as spares for Baghdad.

still on the books of major operators had been kept for specialised reasons such as vehicles converted to open-top or partly for publicity purposes and this is even more the case today. Several operators use historic vehicles on particular routes where their appeal is appropriate, and it thus looks as though there will be no 'final' withdrawal, with these and the many privately preserved examples likely to be seen for many years. A happy thought!

(Left) In their later years, Regent V models passed into an era of unfamiliar names and liveries. This AV470-engined example, ETX 486C, on chassis 2MD3RA623 had started life with Rhondda Transport Co Ltd — an evocative-enough name in the land of valleys and chapels — being one of twelve with Northern Counties forward-entrance 65-seat bodywork dating from 1965. The Rhondda concern was merged with Western Welsh Omnibus Co Ltd and then further mergers led to a change of name to National Welsh Omnibus Services Ltd in April 1978, the fleetname being displayed in Welsh form — Cymru Cenedlaethol — on the offside.

(Below) Meanwhile, the formation of the West Yorkshire Passenger Transport Executive in 1974 led to the adoption of Metro Bradford as the fleetname on this former Bradford Corporation Regent V, YKW 138, seen in a typical local landscape. It was one of 30 on synchromesh-gearbox 30ft. chassis with Metro-Cammell 70-seat bodywork dating from 1963, this particular vehicle being on chassis 2D3RA1207. Whether or not the attempt to apply a 'modern' livery was successful is perhaps a matter of taste, but standards of turn-out had certainly slipped under the pressures of the times, though not aided by the impracticabilities of the new-look front.

The East Kent Road Car Co Ltd, not a Regent user at all until 1958, was to prove the model's largest stronghold by 1980, with 58 still in service. The uniform-looking line-up of Park Royal-bodied Regent V models on the right includes one vehicle from the 1963 delivery, 6804 FN, fourth from the right and having an openable horizontally-divided windscreen. The three nearest buses and the one in the middle date from 1964, there are three 1966 examples at the far end, next to them, one of the final 1968 batch MFN 950F, one of the handful which survive at the time of going to press.

Two of East Kent's last batch of Regents were converted for driver-training duties in 1983 and MFN 948F, on chassis 3D3RA2018, is seen in its yellow livery in February 1986, accompanied by WJG 470J, a Plaxton-bodied AEC Reliance restored to original East Kent crimson and cream livery and owned by the company's canteen social club. The F-registered East Kent Regent V models were the last to be delivered to an English operator, most entering service in December 1967, numerically the last in the D series apart from the Douglas pair, and the only ones with the 3D3RA combination of AV690 engine (albeit derated) and synchromesh gearbox.

Conversions of old double-deckers to open-top virtually became standard policy in many seaside fleets and the Lancaster City Council fleet, which included vehicles taken over from the Morecambe undertaking, was operating KTF 594, this 1949 Regent III (9612E4660) with its Park Royal body thus cut down among its fleet of such vehicles in August 1978. It had fallen into line with the curious Lancaster policy of displaying the registration number digits as the fleet number 594, but had originally been Morecambe No. 65.

Some interesting old buses are still to be seen on mundane duties long after withdrawal from passenger service. London Transport's RT1530 (KGU 290) had already been pensioned off to training duties before the cessation of bus service operation by RT-type vehicles in April 1979, yet it survived within the non-passenger fleet, being seen, a little battered but still basically sound, on skid bus duties at the Chiswick open day in July 1983 when nominally just under 34 years old. The bus at the far end of the group, RT1599, had a similar history while between them is Routemaster RMC1518, one of the former Green Line coach version returned to London Transport again for training and similar duties.

Most of the Regent II models had been scrapped before the bus preservation movement really got under way but fortunately one of the earliest examples, chassis number O6617501, the former London Transport STL2692, had not only gone to a good home with Grimsby Corporation (and then Grimsby-Cleethorpes) after withdrawal from LTE service in 1955 but when it became the last to be pensioned off from that fleet in turn, in January 1968, it was purchased for preservation. It was painstakingly restored to its original green and white livery with red oxide roof and although now becoming quite old even as a preserved vehicle, regularly appears at rallies in the hands of C. Wickens, still looking very smart. It is seen here at Chiswick in July 1983, over 37 years old since it first arrived there from Weymann's and made ready to enter service in January 1946.

Vehicles from one of the top-grade independent operators understandably make an attractive proposition as preserved vehicles. The York Pullman Bus Co Ltd's turn-out was always impressive and here No. 64 (JDN 668), one of the 7.7-litre Regent III models — chassis number 6812A112 — looks very much as it did when first delivered from the bodybuilders, Charles H. Roe Ltd, in March 1954, yet the photograph was taken at Sandtoft in July 1981. The classic four-bay Roe body style was originally given the name Pullman, so is doubly appropriate to this fleet even though by 1954, the window depth was not quite so great as originally.

Reading Corporation had the distinction of placing the last Regent Mark III buses in service when four lowbridge Park Royal-bodied 6812A models entered service in January 1957. Number 4 (MRD 147) was the final vehicle, on chassis 6812A136, and happily it, and the similar No. 3, are still owned by Reading Borough Council. Though powered by the 7.7-litre engine and not the 9.6-litre version built in much greater numbers, it brought to an end the long career of the older unit, first introduced in 1936 in the direct injection A173 form found in these Reading vehicles, and the even older-established AEC crash gearbox. Number 4 is seen here at the 1986 AEC Society rally at Derby.

A ride in the Carris AEC Preservation Group's ex-Lisbon Regent III double-decker is an experience to be savoured by any AEC enthusiast. Number 255, on chassis 9631E1694, was one of sixteen of what by then was CCFL's well-established standard double-deck type, placed in service in 1954. This particular vehicle had covered about 1¼ million miles when taken out of service and brought back to England, when it made a dramatic appearance at the first AEC Society Rally in 1984. Superficially rather shabby — though largely dent-free apart from the front bumper — it soon becomes apparent that this is still basically a very fit bus indeed. The usual Mark III 9.6 preselector noises are all there — though maybe the gearbox note might be a shade 'richer' than when in its youth — and the performance available with intelligent use of the easy gear change still remarkably good even by 1986 standards. The Weymann body seems as solid as ever and of course the view forward in the lower deck can only be described as wierd — a typical provincial Regent III, yet all, including the individual drivers' control apart from the pedals, the 'wrong' way round. With a full load there was considerable body roll on corners in a brisk tour of Derby at the 1986 AEC Rally but this is certainly no feeble relic fit only for static display.

(Below) Tony Peart, long a connoisseur of bus sound effects, brought his crash-gearbox 9.6-litre Regent III, chassis number 9613A5644, to the 1986 AEC Society Rally at Derby. This vehicle has been superbly restored to its original form when placed in service by Doncaster Corporation in June 1951 as number 122. Doncaster was a regular customer for Roe bodywork throughout almost the whole of its career as a bus and trolleybus operator, so the handsome maroon and white livery looked appropriate as well as attractive on this typical Roe 'Pullman' body. In 1955 the bus was sold to local independent G. H. Ennifer Ltd, known as Blue Empire, both operators operating jointly on local routes. A 'demonstration' trip revealed the odd mixture of 9.6-litre and crash gearbox sound effects, the latter with echoes of much earlier models though more subdued than the writer expected; unfortunately worn selector mechanism was causing some difficulty with changes, but this is to be rectified soon.

(Above right) The former Leeds City Transport 30ft. Regent V, 952 JUB, a Monocontrol transmission AV590-powered bus on chassis 2D2RA1579 and dating from 1964, also present at Derby, revealed a different sound symphony. Close one's eyes and riding in it was surprisingly like a journey in a Routemaster — logical, bearing in mind the basic engine and transmission similarity. The wide spring base made stability when cornering not all that inferior, either, markedly less prone to roll than the Lisbon Regent. Somehow the impression of 'crispness' in terms of mechnical condition that the writer used to associate with Leeds buses was still there and the Roe body, as on the Doncaster bus, was also still agreeably solid. It is in original two-tone green though without insignia as yet.

(Right) Another impressive restoration is that of St. Helens Corporation No. 58, a Metro-Cammell-bodied Regent V. It was one of the last Regents built, being based on chassis 2D3RA1975 and entering service in July 1967, only the registration number MDJ 918E giving an external clue to its true age, as St. Helens had some almost identical-looking buses in the 1956-59 period (see page 64). The St. Helens livery as introduced for the RT-type buses shown on page 25 also suited the very different MCW Orion, the positioning of waistbands helping to minimise the high upper-deck waistrail level.

Acknowledgements

This is another book based primarily on personal recollections and contemporary reading going back even beyond the period directly covered. I recall being impressed by pictures of RT1 in the 'Daily Telegraph' in 1939 when I was a 13-year-old schoolboy so the Regent III story in particular could almost be described as a lifelong love affair.

Over such a long period countless people had added to my knowledge, not least my colleagues in AEC's drawing office in 1951-55, when among other things I was in at the birth of the Regent V. More specifically and recently I must again thank Bob Smith and Gordon Baron for assisting with information from official records which underlined, for example, how extensively actual production sequences could depart from numerical chassis number order at times. The PSV Circle and Omnibus Society fleet histories and chassis number lists were, as ever, valuable assemblies of information.

Credit must also be given for the co-operation of Leyland Vehicles Ltd, while Ken Blacker's book 'RT—the story of a London bus' was, as ever, a trusted source, though I hope I have been able to add some fresh perspectives. Keith Beedon contributed some interesting information on Sheffield's views and experiences on transmission design.

The Photocredits list the copyright position on the illustrations used except in a few instances where the origin of illustrations is unknown. However, I would like to thank people who endeavoured to meet detailed requests for photographs covering specific subjects, notably Geoff Atkins, Roy Marshall and Denis Tyler. David Beilby also contributed a very useful collection of prints.

My usual thanks go to the staff at TPC, notably Shirley Gregg for her deciphering of my handwritten copy whilst also coping with the new technology.

Photo credits

Leyland Vehicles Ltd (courtesy BCVM)	All other than those listed below
J. M. Aldridge	46(top), 59(top), 69(top), 73(top), 75(top), 89(centre)
G. F. Ashwell	11(bottom)
G. H. F. Atkins	12(top), 14(top), 31(top), 35(centre), 39(bottom), 45(bottom), 46(bottom), 49(top & bottom), 53(centre), 84(top), 90(all)
D. Beilby collection	71(bottom), 74(both), 76(bottom), 92(both)
Brush Coachworks Ltd/TPC	11(top)
J. Cockshott	86(top right)
C. R. L. Coles	25(top right)
A. A. Cooper	20(bottom), 61(top)
J. E. Cull	9(bottom)
R. C. Davis	11(centre right)
M. Fowler	89(bottom)
B. V. Franey	8
J. C. Gillham	68(bottom)
Greater Manchester PTE/TPC	60(top)
R. N. Hannay collection	32(top), 43(bottom), 59(bottom), 60(bottom), 70(top), 87(bottom)
Hestair Duple Ltd	34(top)
B. A. Jenkins	59(centre), 86(bottom)
A. D. Jack	83(bottom)
A. E. Jones	76(top right)
T. W. W. Knowles	93(top)
London Regional Transport	5, 21(bottom)
R. F. Mack	13(bottom), 85(bottom)

R. Marshall	11(centre left), 29(bottom left), 33(top left), 45(top), 49(centre), 58(both top), 63(top right), 72(bottom), 86(top left), 91(top)
Merseyside PTE	32(bottom), 57(top), 88(top)
Metro-Cammell Weymann Ltd	68(top)
R. A. Mills	7(bottom), 14(bottom)
M. Montano (TPC collection)	67(bottom)
R. L. Moore	53(bottom)
S. A. Newman	47(bottom)
Northern Coachbuilders Ltd	35(top)
D. A. Peart	84(bottom)
H. Piltz	Front cover
F. G. Reynolds	17(top), 25(centre), 36(top), 48(top), 85(top), 89(top)
J. A. Senior	Rear cover
M. S. Stokes	73(centre), 93(second bottom)
A. A. Townsin	22(both bottom), 59(top left), 65(bottom), 66(top), 76(top left), 78(both), 79(top), 94(bottom), 95(all)
A. A. Townsin collection	3, 22(centre), 25(top left), 28(top right), 29(bottom right), 31(bottom right), 43(centre right), 48(both lower), 70(bottom), 85(centre right)
D. L. Tyler	20(centre), 33(top right), 52(top), 94(top & centre)
Tyne & Wear PTE	36(bottom)
G. Walker	10(top)
D. Wayman	73(bottom), 93(second top & bottom)
A. M. Wright	56(top), 85(centre left)